Illinois Central College
Learning Resources Center

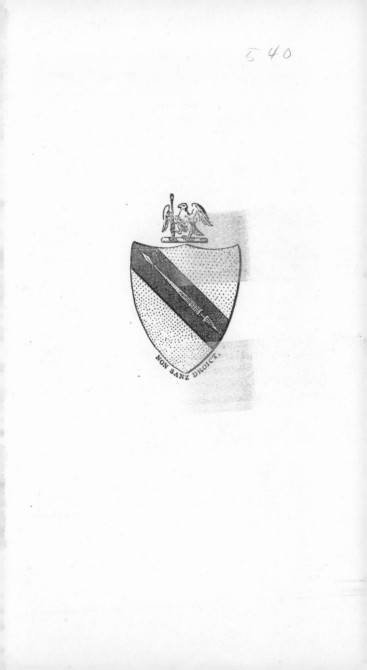

NON SANZ DROICT.

William Shakespeare

The Tragedy of
TITUS ANDRONICUS

EDITED BY
Sylvan Barnet

The Signet Classic Shakespeare
GENERAL EDITOR: SYLVAN BARNET

PUBLISHED BY THE NEW AMERICAN LIBRARY, NEW YORK
AND
THE NEW ENGLISH LIBRARY LIMITED, LONDON

PR
2835
.A2
B3

SHAKESPEARE
Titus
NAL

First Printing, February, 1964

SIGNET TRADEMARK REG. U.S. PAT. OFF. AND FOREIGN COUNTRIES
REGISTERED TRADEMARK—MARCA REGISTRADA
HECHO EN CHICAGO, U.S.A.

SIGNET CLASSICS *are published by*
The New American Library of World Literature, Inc.
501 Madison Avenue, New York, New York 10022

PRINTED IN THE UNITED STATES OF AMERICA

SHAKESPEARE
Titus
NAL

First Printing, February, 1964

SIGNET CLASSICS *are published by*
The New American Library of World Literature, Inc.
501 Madison Avenue, New York, New York 10022

PRINTED IN THE UNITED STATES OF AMERICA

Contents

Shakespeare: Prefatory Remarks

Between the record of his baptism in Stratford on 26 April 1564 and the record of his burial in Stratford on 25 April 1616, some forty documents name Shakespeare, and many others name his parents, his children, and his grandchildren. More facts are known about William Shakespeare than about any other playwright of the period except Ben Jonson. The facts should, however, be distinguished from the legends. The latter, inevitably more engaging and better known, tell us that the Stratford boy killed a calf in high style, poached deer and rabbits, and was forced to flee to London, where he held horses outside a playhouse. These traditions are only traditions; they may be true, but no evidence supports them, and it is well to stick to the facts.

Mary Arden, the dramatist's mother, was the daughter of a substantial landowner; about 1557 she married John Shakespeare, who was a glove-maker and trader in various farm commodities. In 1557 John Shakespeare was a member of the Council (the governing body of Stratford), in 1558 a constable of the borough, in 1561 one of the two town chamberlains, in 1565 an alderman (entitling him to the appellation "Mr."), in 1568 high bailiff—the town's highest political office, equivalent to mayor. After 1577, for an unknown reason he drops out of local politics. The birthday of William Shakespeare, the eldest son of this locally prominent man, is unrecorded; but the Stratford parish register records that the infant was baptized on 26 April 1564. (It is quite possible that he was born on 23 April, but this date has probably been assigned by tradition because it is the date on which, fifty-two years later, he died.) The attendance records of the Stratford grammar school of the period are not extant, but it is reasonable to assume that the son of a local official attended the school and received substantial training in Latin. The masters of the school from Shakespeare's seventh to fifteenth years held Oxford degrees; the Elizabethan curriculum excluded mathematics and the natural sciences but taught a good deal of Latin rhetoric, logic, and literature. On 27 November 1582 a marriage license was issued to Shakespeare and Anne Hathaway, eight years his senior. The couple had a child in May, 1583. Perhaps the marriage was necessary, but perhaps the couple had earlier engaged in a formal "troth plight" which would render their children legitimate even if no further ceremony were performed. In 1585 Anne Hathaway bore Shakespeare twins.

That Shakespeare was born is excellent; that he married and had children is pleasant; but that we know nothing about his departure from Stratford to London, or about the beginning of his theatrical career, is lamentable and must be admitted. We would gladly sacrifice details about his children's baptism for details about his earliest days on the stage. Perhaps the poaching episode is true (but it is first reported almost a century after Shakespeare's death), or perhaps he first left Stratford to be a schoolteacher, as another tradition holds; perhaps he was moved by

> Such wind as scatters young men through the world,
> To seek their fortunes further than at home
> Where small experience grows.

In 1592, thanks to the cantankerousness of Robert Greene, a rival playwright and a pamphleteer, we have our first reference, a snarling one, to Shakespeare as an actor and playwright. Greene warns those of his own educated friends who wrote for the theater against an actor who has presumed to turn playwright:

> There is an upstart crow, beautified with our feathers, that with his *tiger's heart wrapped in a player's hide* supposes

he is as well able to bombast out a blank verse as the best
of you, and being an absolute Johannes-factotum is in his
own conceit the only Shake-scene in a country.

The reference to the player, as well as the allusion to
Aesop's crow (who strutted in borrowed plumage, as an
actor struts in fine words not his own), makes it clear that
by this date Shakespeare had both acted and written. That
Shakespeare is meant is indicated not only by "Shake-
scene" but by the parody of a line from one of Shakespeare's
plays, *3 Henry VI:* "O, tiger's heart wrapped in a woman's
hide." If Shakespeare in 1592 was prominent enough to be
attacked by an envious dramatist, he probably had served
an apprenticeship in the theater for at least a few years.

In any case, by 1592 Shakespeare had acted and written,
and there are a number of subsequent references to him as
an actor: documents indicate that in 1598 he is a "principal
comedian," in 1603 a "principal tragedian," in 1608 he is
one of the "men players." The profession of actor was not
for a gentleman, and it occasionally drew the scorn of
university men who resented writing speeches for persons
less educated than themselves, but it was respectable
enough: players, if prosperous, were in effect members of
the bourgeoisie, and there is nothing to suggest that Stratford considered William Shakespeare less than a solid citizen. When, in 1596, the Shakespeares were granted a coat
of arms, the grant was made to Shakespeare's father, but
probably William Shakespeare (who the next year bought
the second-largest house in town) had arranged the matter
on his own behalf. In subsequent transactions he is occasionally styled a gentleman.

Although in 1593 and 1594 Shakespeare published two
narrative poems dedicated to the Earl of Southampton,
Venus and Adonis and *The Rape of Lucrece,* and may well
have written most or all of his sonnets in the middle nineties,
Shakespeare's literary activity seems to have been almost
entirely devoted to the theater. (It may be significant that
the two narrative poems were written in years when the
plague closed the theaters for several months.) In 1594 he
was a charter member of a theatrical company called the

Chamberlain's Men (which in 1603 changed its name to the King's Men); until he retired to Stratford (about 1611, apparently), he was with this remarkably stable company. From 1599 the company acted primarily at the Globe Theatre, in which Shakespeare held a one-tenth interest. Other Elizabethan dramatists are known to have acted, but no other is known also to have been entitled to a share in the profits of the playhouse.

Shakespeare's first eight published plays did not have his name on them, but this is not remarkable; the most popular play of the sixteenth century, Thomas Kyd's *The Spanish Tragedy,* went through many editions without naming Kyd, and Kyd's authorship is known only because a book on the profession of acting happens to quote (and attribute to Kyd) some lines on the interest of Roman emperors in the drama. What is remarkable is that after 1598 Shakespeare's name commonly appears on printed plays—some of which are not his. Another indication of his popularity comes from Francis Meres, author of *Palladis Tamia: Wit's Treasury* (1598): in this anthology of snippets accompanied by an essay on literature, many playwrights are mentioned, but Shakespeare's name occurs more often than any other, and Shakespeare is the only playwright whose plays are listed.

From his acting, playwriting, and share in a theater, Shakespeare seems to have made considerable money. He put it to work, making substantial investments in Stratford real estate. When he made his will (less than a month before he died), he sought to leave his property intact to his descendants. Of small bequests to relatives and to friends (including three actors, Richard Burbage, John Heminges, and Henry Condell), that to his wife of the second-best bed has provoked the most comment; perhaps it was the bed the couple had slept in, the best being reserved for visitors. In any case, had Shakespeare not excepted it, the bed would have gone (with the rest of his household possessions) to his daughter and her husband. On 25 April 1616 he was buried within the chancel of the church at Stratford. An unattractive monument to his memory, placed on a wall near the grave, says he died on 23 April. Over the grave itself are the lines, perhaps by Shakespeare, that (more than his literary fame) have kept his bones undisturbed in the crowded burial ground where old bones were often dislodged to make way for new:

> Good friend, for Jesus' sake forbear
> To dig the dust enclosèd here.
> Blessed be the man that spares these stones
> And cursed be he that moves my bones.

Thirty-seven plays, as well as some nondramatic poems, are held to constitute the Shakespeare canon. The dates of composition of most of the works are highly uncertain, but there is often evidence of a *terminus a quo* (starting point) and/or a *terminus ad quem* (terminal point) that provides a framework for intelligent guessing. For example, *Richard II* cannot be earlier than 1595, the publication date of some material to which it is indebted; *The Merchant of Venice* cannot be later than 1598, the year Francis Meres mentioned it. Sometimes arguments for a date hang on an alleged topical allusion, such as the lines about the unseasonable weather in *A Midsummer Night's Dream,* II.i.81–87, but such an allusion (if indeed it is an allusion) can be variously interpreted, and in any case there is always the possibility that a topical allusion was inserted during a revision, years after the composition of a play. Dates are often attributed on the basis of style, and although conjectures about style usually rest on other conjectures, sooner or later one must rely on one's literary sense. There is no real proof, for example, that *Othello* is not as early as *Romeo and Juliet,* but one feels *Othello* is later, and because the first record of its performance is 1604, one is glad enough to set its composition at that date and not push it back into Shakespeare's early years. The following chronology, then, is as much indebted to informed guesswork and sensitivity as it is to fact. The dates, necessarily imprecise, indicate something like a scholarly consensus.

PLAYS

1588–93	*The Comedy of Errors*
1588–94	*Love's Labor's Lost*

1590–91	*2 Henry VI*
1590–91	*3 Henry VI*
1591–92	*1 Henry VI*
1592–93	*Richard III*
1592–94	*Titus Andronicus*
1593–94	*The Taming of the Shrew*
1593–95	*The Two Gentlemen of Verona*
1594–96	*Romeo and Juliet*
1595	*Richard II*
1594–96	*A Midsummer Night's Dream*
1596–97	*King John*
1596–97	*The Merchant of Venice*
1597	*1 Henry IV*
1597–98	*2 Henry IV*
1598–1600	*Much Ado About Nothing*
1598–99	*Henry V*
1599	*Julius Caesar*
1599–1600	*As You Like It*
1599–1600	*Twelfth Night*
1600–01	*Hamlet*
1597–1601	*The Merry Wives of Windsor*
1601–02	*Troilus and Cressida*
1602–04	*All's Well That Ends Well*
1603–04	*Othello*
1604	*Measure for Measure*
1605–06	*King Lear*
1605–06	*Macbeth*
1606–07	*Antony and Cleopatra*
1605–08	*Timon of Athens*
1607–09	*Coriolanus*
1608–09	*Pericles*
1609–10	*Cymbeline*
1610–11	*The Winter's Tale*
1611	*The Tempest*
1612–13	*Henry VIII*

POEMS

| 1592 | *Venus and Adonis* |
| 1593–94 | *The Rape of Lucrece* |

Shakespeare's Theater

In Shakespeare's infancy, Elizabethan actors performed wherever they could—in great halls, at court, in the courtyards of inns. The innyards must have made rather unsatisfactory theaters: on some days they were unavailable because carters bringing goods to London used them as depots; when available, they had to be rented from the innkeeper; perhaps most important, London inns were subject to the Common Council of London, which was not well disposed toward theatricals. In 1574 the Common Council required that plays and playing places in London be licensed. It asserted that

> sundry great disorders and inconveniences have been found to ensue to this city by the inordinate haunting of great multitudes of people, specially youth, to plays, interludes, and shows, namely occasion of frays and quarrels, evil practices of incontinency in great inns having chambers and secret places adjoining to their open stages and galleries,

and ordered that innkeepers who wished licenses to hold performances put up a bond and make contributions to the poor.

The requirement that plays and innyard theaters be licensed, along with the other drawbacks of playing at inns, probably drove James Burbage (a carpenter-turned-actor) to rent in 1576 a plot of land northeast of the city walls and to build here—on property outside the jurisdiction of the city—England's first permanent construction designed for plays. He called it simply the Theatre. About all that is known of its construction is that it was wood. It soon had imitators, the most famous being the Globe (1599), built across the Thames (again outside the city's jurisdiction), out of timbers of the Theatre, which had been dismantled when Burbage's lease ran out.

There are three important sources of information about the structure of Elizabethan playhouses—drawings, a contract, and stage directions in plays. Of drawings, only the so-called De Witt drawing (c. 1596) of the Swan—really a friend's copy of De Witt's drawing—is of much significance. It shows a building of three tiers, with a stage jutting from a wall into the yard or center of the building. The tiers are roofed, and part of the stage is covered by a roof that projects from the rear and is supported at its front on two posts, but the groundlings, who paid a penny to stand in front of the stage, were exposed to the sky. (Performances in such a playhouse were held only in the daytime; artificial illumination was not used.) At the rear of the stage are two doors; above the stage is a gallery. The second major source of information, the contract for the Fortune, specifies that although the Globe is to be the model, the Fortune is to be square, eighty feet outside and fifty-five inside. The stage is to be forty-three feet broad, and is to extend into the middle of the yard (i.e., it is twenty-seven and a half feet deep). For patrons willing to pay more than the general admission charged of the groundlings, there were to be three galleries provided with seats. From the third chief source, stage directions, one learns that entrance to the stage was by doors, presumably spaced widely apart at the rear ("Enter one citizen at one door, and another at the other"), and that in addition to the platform stage there was occasionally some sort of curtained booth or alcove allowing for "discovery" scenes, and some sort of playing space "aloft" or "above" to represent (for example) the top of a city's walls or a room above the street. Doubtless each theater had its own peculiarities, but perhaps we can talk about a "typical" Elizabethan theater if we realize that no theater need exactly have fit the description, just as no father is the typical father with 3.7 children. This hypothetical theater is wooden, round or polygonal (in *Henry V* Shakespeare calls it a "wooden *O*"), capable of holding some eight hundred spectators standing in the yard around the projecting elevated stage and some fifteen hundred additional spectators seated in the three roofed galleries. The stage, protected by a "shadow" or "heavens" or roof, is entered by two doors; behind the doors is the "tiring house" (attiring house, i.e., dressing room), and above the doors is some sort of gallery that may sometimes hold spectators but that can be used (for example) as the bedroom from which Romeo—according to a stage direction in one text—"goeth down." Some evidence suggests that a throne can be lowered onto the platform stage, perhaps from the "shadow"; certainly characters can descend from the stage through a trap or traps into the cellar or "hell." Sometimes this space beneath the platform accommodates a sound-effects man or musician (in *Antony and Cleopatra* "music of the hautboys is under the stage") or an actor (in *Hamlet* the "Ghost cries under the stage"). Most characters simply walk on and off, but because there is no curtain in front of the platform, corpses will have to be carried off (Hamlet must lug Polonius' guts into the neighbor room), or will have to fall at the rear, where the curtain on the alcove or booth can be drawn to conceal them.

Such may have been the so-called "public theater." Another kind of theater, called the "private theater" because its much greater admission charge limited its audience to the wealthy or the prodigal, must be briefly mentioned. The private theater was basically a large room, entirely roofed and therefore artificially illuminated, with a stage at one end. In 1576 one such theater was established in Blackfriars, a Dominican priory in London that had been suppressed in 1538 and confiscated by the Crown and thus was not under the city's jurisdiction. All the actors in the Blackfriars theater were boys about eight to thirteen years old (in the public theaters similar boys played female parts; a boy Lady Macbeth played to a man Macbeth). This private theater had a precarious existence, and ceased operations in 1584. In 1596 James Burbage, who had already made theatrical history by building the Theatre, began to construct a second Blackfriars theater. He died in 1597, and for several years this second Blackfriars theater was used by a troupe of boys, but in 1608 two of Burbage's sons and five other actors (including Shakespeare) became joint operators of the theater, using it in the winter when the open-air Globe was unsuitable. Perhaps such a smaller theater, roofed, artificially illuminated, and with a tradition of a courtly audience, exerted an influence on Shakespeare's late plays.

Performances in the private theaters may well have had intermissions during which music was played, but in the public theaters the action was probably uninterrupted, flowing from scene to scene almost without a break. Actors would enter, speak, exit, and others would immediately enter and establish (if necessary) the new locale by a few properties and by words and gestures. Here are some samples of Shakespeare's scene painting:

> This is Illyria, lady.

> Well, this is the Forest of Arden.

> This castle hath a pleasant seat; the air
> Nimbly and sweetly recommends itself
> Unto our gentle senses.

On the other hand, it is a mistake to conceive of the Elizabethan stage as bare. Although Shakespeare's Chorus in *Henry V* calls the stage an "unworthy scaffold" and urges the spectators to "eke out our performance with your mind," there was considerable spectacle. The last act of *Macbeth,* for example, has five stage directions calling for "drum and colors," and another sort of appeal to the eye is indicated by the stage direction "Enter Macduff, with Macbeth's head." Some scenery and properties may have been substantial; doubtless a throne was used, and in one play of the period we encounter this direction: "Hector takes up a great piece of rock and casts at Ajax, who tears up a young tree by the roots and assails Hector." The matter is of some importance, and will be glanced at again in the next section.

The Texts of Shakespeare

Though eighteen of his plays were published during his lifetime, Shakespeare seems never to have supervised their publication. There is nothing unusual here; when a playwright sold a play to a theatrical company he surrendered his ownership of it. Normally a company would not publish the play, because to publish it meant to allow competitors to acquire the piece. Some plays, however, did get published; apparently treacherous actors sometimes pieced together a play for a publisher, sometimes a company in need of money sold a play, and sometimes a company allowed a play to be published that no longer drew audiences. That Shakespeare did not concern himself with publication, then, is scarcely remarkable; of his contemporaries only Ben Jonson carefully supervised the publication of his own plays. In 1623, seven years after Shakespeare's death, John Heminges and Henry Condell (two senior members of Shakespeare's company, who had performed with him for about twenty years) collected his plays—published and unpublished—into a large volume, commonly called the First Folio. (A folio is a volume consisting of sheets that have been folded once, each sheet thus making two leaves, or four pages. The eighteen plays published during Shakespeare's lifetime had been issued one play per volume in small books called quartos. Each sheet in a quarto has been folded twice, making four leaves, or eight pages.) The First Folio contains thirty-six plays; a thirty-seventh, *Pericles,* though not in the Folio, is regarded as canonical. Heminges and Condell suggest in an address "To the great variety of readers" that the republished plays are presented in better form than in the quartos: "Before you were abused with diverse stolen and surreptitious copies, maimed and deformed by the frauds and stealths of injurious impostors that exposed them; even those, are now offered to your view cured and perfect of their limbs, and all the rest absolute in their numbers, as he [i.e., Shakespeare] conceived them."

Whoever was assigned to prepare the texts for publication in the First Folio seems to have taken his job seriously and yet not to have performed it with uniform care. The sources of the texts seem to have been, in general, good unpublished copies or the best published copies. The first play in the collection, *The Tempest,* is divided into acts and scenes, has unusually full stage directions and descriptions of spectacle, and concludes with a list of the characters, but the editor was not able (or willing) to present all of the succeeding texts so fully dressed. Later texts occasionally show signs of carelessness: in one scene of *Much Ado About Nothing* the names of actors, instead of characters, appear as speech prefixes, as they had in the quarto, which the Folio reprints; proofreading throughout the Folio is spotty and apparently was done without reference to the printer's copy; the pagination of *Hamlet* jumps from 156 to 257.

A modern editor of Shakespeare must first select his copy; no problem if the play exists only in the Folio, but a considerable problem if the relationship between a quarto and the Folio—or an early quarto and a later one—is unclear. When an editor has chosen what seems to him to be the most authoritative text or texts for his copy, he has not done with making decisions. First of all, he must reckon with Elizabethan spelling. If he is not producing a facsimile, he probably modernizes it, but ought he to preserve the old form of words that apparently were pronounced quite unlike their modern forms—"lanthorn" "alablaster"? If he preserves these forms, is he really preserving Shakespeare's forms or perhaps those of a compositor in the printing house? What is one to do when one finds "lanthorn" and "lantern" in adjacent lines? (The editors of this series in general, but not invariably, assume that words should be spelled in their modern form.) Elizabethan punctuation, too, presents problems. For example in the First Folio, the only text for the play, Macbeth rejects his wife's idea that he can wash the blood from his hand:

> no: this my Hand will rather
> The multitudinous Seas incarnardine,
> Making the Greene one, Red.

Obviously an editor will remove the superfluous capitals, and he will probably alter the spelling to "incarnadine," but will he leave the comma before "red," letting Macbeth speak of the sea as "the green one," or will he (like most modern editors) remove the comma and thus have Macbeth say that his hand will make the ocean *uniformly* red?

An editor will sometimes have to change more than spelling or punctuation. Macbeth says to his wife:

> I dare do all that may become a man,
> Who dares no more, is none.

For two centuries editors have agreed that the second line is unsatisfactory, and have emended "no" to "do": "Who dares do more is none." But when in the same play Ross says that fearful persons

> floate vpon a wilde and violent Sea
> Each way, and moue,

need "move" be emended to "none," as it often is, on the hunch that the compositor misread the manuscript? The editors of the Signet Classic Shakespeare have restrained themselves from making abundant emendations. In their minds they hear Dr. Johnson on the dangers of emending: "I have adopted the Roman sentiment, that it is more honorable to save a citizen than to kill an enemy." Some departures (in addition to spelling, punctuation, and lineation) from the copy text have of course been made, but the original readings are listed in a note following the play, so that the reader can evaluate them for himself.

The editors of the Signet Classic Shakespeare, following tradition, have added line numbers and in many cases act and scene divisions as well as indications of locale at the beginning of scenes. The Folio divided most of the plays into acts and some into scenes. Early eighteenth-century editors increased the divisions. These divisions, which provide a convenient way of referring to passages in the plays, have been retained, but when not in the text chosen as the basis for the Signet Classic text they are enclosed in square brackets [ ] to indicate that they are editorial additions. Similarly, although no play of Shakespeare's published during his lifetime was equipped with indications of locale at the heads of scene divisions, locales have here been added in square brackets for the convenience of the reader, who lacks the information afforded to spectators by costumes, properties, and gestures. The spectator can tell at a glance he is in the throne room, but without an editorial indication the reader may be puzzled for a while. It should be mentioned, incidentally, that there are a few authentic stage directions—perhaps Shakespeare's, perhaps a prompter's—that suggest locales: for example, "Enter Brutus in his orchard," and "They go up into the Senate house." It is hoped that the bracketed additions provide the reader with the sort of help provided in these two authentic directions, but it is equally hoped that the reader will remember that the stage was not loaded with scenery.

No editor during the course of his work can fail to recollect some words Heminges and Condell prefixed to the Folio:

> It had been a thing, we confess, worthy to have been wished, that the author himself had lived to have set forth and overseen his own writings. But since it hath been ordained otherwise, and he by death departed from the right, we pray you do not envy his friends the office of their care and pain to have collected and published them.

Nor can an editor, after he has done his best, forget Heminges and Condell's final words: "And so we leave you to other of his friends, whom if you need can be your guides. If you need them not, you can lead yourselves, and others. And such readers we wish him."

SYLVAN BARNET
Tufts University

Introduction

Titus Andronicus has had few admirers and numerous detractors. T. S. Eliot states the detractors' case as directly as any: *Titus* is "one of the stupidest and most uninspired plays ever written, a play in which it is incredible that Shakespeare had any hand at all, a play in which the best passages would be too highly honored by the signature of Peele." Unlike Eliot's notably original view that *Hamlet* "so far from being Shakespeare's masterpiece . . . is most certainly an artistic failure," his remark on *Titus* is a commonplace: Dr. Johnson, Hazlitt, Coleridge, and the editor of the Yale edition denied Shakespeare's authorship of most of the play; the editor of the New Cambridge edition gives much of it to Peele and saves some of the Shakespearean passages only by the desperate expedient of claiming that they are not really bad but are a clever burlesque of bad writing.

The idea that *Titus* may not be entirely Shakespeare's is at least as old as 1687, when Thomas Ravenscroft, who had recently given the stage his adaptation of the play, recorded that he had been told that Shakespeare "only gave some master-touches to one or two of the principal parts or characters." But the evidence that Shakespeare wrote *Titus* is weighty. In 1598 Francis Meres listed it as one of Shakespeare's plays, and in 1623 Heminges and Condell, who had acted with Shakespeare for some twenty years, included *Titus* in the Folio collection of his plays. However displeased we may be by part or all of *Titus*, there is no evidence that it is not his.

There are, of course, some inconsistencies that have been offered as proof that Shakespeare was revising an older play. We are told in II.iii.86 that Tamora's infidelity to the Emperor has "made him noted [i.e., notorious] long," although Tamora and the Emperor have been married only one night. But such an inconsistency proves no more about dual authorship than the similar treatment of time in *Othello*, or the apparently contradictory remarks about Macbeth's children. More serious is the shift of the villain's role from Tamora to Aaron, but again it does not prove that Shakespeare is revising an earlier play; probably he found the Moor Aaron coming to life as he worked on him, and Tamora simply fell into the background until the last act, when her part is stronger.

There is no sense trying to dissociate Shakespeare from *Titus;* all the available evidence insists that it is canonical. But neither is there any sense in emphasizing, as has recently been done, its connection with Shakespeare's early historical plays or with his later Roman tragedies. A good deal has been written about the Elizabethan history play as a dramatized sermon on the wounds of civil war, a sermon of special interest to Englishmen whose monarch was an aging and heirless queen. The later Roman plays, too, are seen to have political subjects. It is true, of course, that *Julius Caesar, Antony and Cleopatra,* and *Coriolanus* are all concerned in part with civil war, but it is hard to believe that while witnessing a performance of, say, *Antony and Cleopatra,* Shakespeare's audience fretted about the possibility that England would find itself the battlefield of triumvirs; rather it must have been watching with interest a story in which political themes are subordinated to the doings of a "lass unparalleled" and a general who becomes "the noble ruin of her magic." *Titus* does indeed concern itself, in part of the first scene, with establishing the succession in Rome; Titus is asked (I.i.186) to "help to set a head on headless Rome." But thereafter the motif fades from view until the fifth act, when Lucius, one of Titus' sons, leads an army against the vicious emperor whom Titus in the first scene helped to establish. In V.iii.67 ff. there is a speech stressing the horror of civil war, but it can scarcely be said to be closely related to what has preceded it, and its ascription to a nameless "Roman Lord" suggests that it may well have been an afterthought. There is, furthermore, a curious bit of evidence that Shakespeare regarded the play as less political than did the earliest recorded interpreter, the printer or editor of the second quarto (1600). The first quarto (1594) concludes—as presumably Shakespeare concluded—with some lines about the deceased wicked queen:

> As for that ravenous tiger, Tamora,
> No funeral rite, nor man in mourning weed,
> No mournful bell shall ring her burial;
> But throw her forth to beasts and birds to prey.
> Her life was beastly and devoid of pity,
> And being dead, let birds on her take pity.

When a second edition was called for, it was apparently set up from a copy that had suffered some damage to the foot of the last leaf of text; the person overseeing the publication seems to have mistakenly thought that some lines had been lost at the foot, though in fact nothing was lost but "Finis the Tragedy of Titus Andronicus." He added four lines:

> See justice done on Aaron, that damned Moor,
> By whom our heavy haps had their beginning;
> Then afterwards to order well the state,
> That like events may ne'er it ruinate.

The last two lines, though bad, are appropriate enough and have their parallels in later plays when rather colorless characters assure their fellows that some sort of order is returning to the state, but certainly neither these lines nor the first scene should turn our minds from characters and passions to politics. Shakespeare himself ended the play by calling attention not to political concerns but to

the pitiless queen whose body will be left for scavenging
birds.

To say that Shakespeare ended his play with a comment on the Queen and not on the state is not to deny
that there are substantial passages devoted to the state.
But the final lines emphasize the central concern of the
play—the passions and deeds that are the stuff of tragedy.
Critics tend to suggest that we go to a tragedy so that
we may draw political and ethical conclusions, but the
tragic dramatists tend to emphasize deeds of horror and
passionate responses to these deeds. Even at the end of
a play, the emphasis is not on drawing conclusions, but
on experiencing emotions. Nobody who witnesses *Hamlet*
can feel that the entrance of Fortinbras shifts attention
from tragic experiences to ethics and politics; attention
is kept on the catastrophic happenings in Denmark.

Ambassador.   The sight is dismal;
    And our affairs from England come too late.
    The ears are senseless that should give us hearing. . . .

Horatio. But since, so jump upon this bloody question,
    You from the Polack wars, and you from England,
    Are here arrived, give order that these bodies
    High on a stage be placèd to the view,
    And let me speak to th' yet unknowing world
    How these things came about. So shall you hear
    Of carnal, bloody, and unnatural acts,
    Of accidental judgments, casual slaughters,
    Of deaths put on by cunning and forced cause,
    And, in this upshot, purposes mistook
    Fall'n on th' inventors' heads.
                                    (*Hamlet* V.ii. 368–86)

The violence of *Titus* has often aroused condemnation,
as though tragedy did not customarily dramatize violence.
It is true that *Titus* has more than its share, but if, for
example, we find especially abhorrent the introduction
of the severed heads of two of Titus' sons, it is perhaps
because we have forgotten (since directors customarily
omit the business) a stage direction in the last act of

Macbeth, "Enter Macduff, with Macbeth's head." Repulsive happenings are not something Shakespeare dramatized in his youth and then outgrew; *Hamlet* concludes with four corpses (there would be a fifth if Horatio had his way), to say nothing of the earlier deaths or the skulls the gravediggers unearth; *King Lear* calls for Gloucester to be blinded before the audience, and it concludes with the (to modern taste) gratuitous introduction of the corpses of Goneril and Regan, who have had the grace to die offstage. The dozen or so deaths in *Titus* are about double the number in *Lear,* and the rape and cannibalism in Titus are unparalleled elsewhere in Shakespeare, but they are not incompatible with the idea of tragedy. Nor are they mere Elizabethan sensationalism. If we recall Clytemnestra exulting over her slaughtered husband, or the incestuous Oedipus entering on the stage with bloody eyeless sockets, or the lecherous Pentheus, whose mother will in a frenzy exult over his severed head, we remember that none of the world's four great tragic dramatists shrinks from dramatizing the demonic and the horrible. We tend, especially if we are readers rather than spectators, to emphasize the wisdom and patience that are allegedly achieved through heroic suffering, but surely we ought to recall, for example, that Hamlet in the last act forces poison down Claudius' throat. Again, we can talk of purgation and reconciliation in *King Lear,* but we must recall that the cries and horrors do not disappear toward the end of the play; it is only seventy-five lines before the end that Lear enters with the dead Cordelia in his arms ("Howl, howl, howl, howl"), and the play closes with a dead march.

Of Shakespeare's early tragedies—*Richard III, Titus, Richard II,* and *Romeo and Juliet*—*Titus* is certainly the poorest, but it alone has a protagonist who is both noble and flawed, and thus it looks forward to *Julius Caesar* and to the greater tragedies. *Romeo and Juliet,* perhaps the best of Shakespeare's early tragedies, is an incomparably finer piece of work than *Titus,* but its vision of star-crossed lovers is quite different from the tragic vision of *Hamlet, Othello, Lear, Macbeth, Antony and Cleopatra,* and

Coriolanus, whose protagonists in a significant way resemble Titus. In *Romeo and Juliet* the lack of any vigorous presentation of evil (in most of the greater tragedies Shakespeare did not hesitate to draw potent villains), the decisive role played by chance, the youth and innocence of the lovers, and the emphasis on reconciliation at the end, all work together to produce a tragedy that strikes us as substantially different from the later tragedies. Of course one can say that the lovers are in some measure responsible for their fates—if they had not loved they might have outlived their parents—but the overall impression is one of innocence destroyed by destiny and released from this transitory world to a timeless realm. *Titus* is something else; in it, as in the great tragedies, deeds recoil on the head of the doers and even well-intentioned deeds may have their painful consequences. Titus offers up Alarbus as a sacrifice to the souls of the dead, and he thereby incurs the hatred of Tamora. Declining to accept the title of emperor, Titus helps to establish Saturninus, who quickly proves to be his foe. Titus nominates Saturninus apparently because he is the elder son—a reasonable basis—but the first two speeches of the play suggest to the hearer that Bassianus rather than Saturninus is the fitter. What Shakespeare is doing, of course, is dramatizing what seems to be an essential tragic fact—a man doing something according to his best lights and according to an impressive but, as it proves, mistaken code. In his dealings with his sons, as well as with Tamora and Saturninus, Titus prefigures the great tragic heroes: Titus' inflexible conception of honor alienates him even from those he loves. He moves, a Titan, in a world of his own, at times heroically silent when lesser men would weep, at times loudly lamenting to the stones, when lesser men would be silent. At the start it is said of him,

> A nobler man, a braver warrior,
> Lives not this day within the city walls.

> (I.i.25–26)

His nobility, his bravery, sets him off from others, even from his own sons, and (like Othello's high vision of Desdemona that leads him to kill her when he thinks her unchaste) Titus' virtues themselves become oppressive. His code of honor sets him apart from other men; he becomes increasingly aware of a painful isolation, and he speaks of it grandly, as a tragic hero should. Juliet comes to realize that her "dismal scene [she] needs must act alone"; Macbeth, plotting Banquo's death, keeps even his wife "innocent of the knowledge"; Hamlet speaks "wild and whirling words" and is markedly detached from Horatio, as well as from Claudius, Gertrude, and Ophelia; Lear will "abjure all roofs"; Coriolanus, told that he is banished from Rome, will reply "I banish you." Titus, the earliest of these protagonists, says of himself:

> For now I stand as one upon a rock,
> Environed with a wilderness of sea,
> Who marks the waxing tide grow wave by wave,
> Expecting ever when some envious surge
> Will in his brinish bowels swallow him.
> This way to death my wretched sons are gone,
> Here stands my other son, a banished man,
> And here my brother weeping at my woes:
> But that which gives my soul the greatest spurn
> Is dear Lavinia, dearer than my soul.
>
> (III.i.93–102)

Like Shakespeare's other tragic figures, he wears the shirt of Nessus and gives vent to his feelings. The speech is a little too self-conscious, the assonance, alliteration, and other repetitions are a little too insistent (*waxing, wave by wave; expecting, ever, envious; brinish bowels; stands, son; weeping, woes; soul, spurn, dear, dearer, soul*), but one would be hard pressed to point to a better passage in the work of any of Shakespeare's early contemporaries other than Marlowe.

Shakespeare must have felt that his chief problem was one of style, not of plot: What sort of rhetoric could effectively present the bloody and unnatural horrors that were the substance of Elizabethan tragedy and of classical tragedy as he knew it? There was, of course, no question of presenting tragic happenings "realistically"; tragedy was concerned with unusual people in unusual situations; its medium was verse, not prose. *Titus* contains a few brief exchanges in prose, and indeed the Clown's prose is notable ("God forbid I should be so bold to press to heaven in my young days"), but when he wrote *Titus,* Shakespeare must have been unable to conceive of the significant role that prose might play in his tragedies. Even half a century or so after Shakespeare's great achievements in tragic prose, England's best dramatic critic of the time believed that because tragedy shows us "nature wrought up to a higher pitch" it ought to be in verse. (Dryden advocated heroic couplets, however, not blank verse.) The verse drama of Shakespeare's infancy and much of that of his youth was rhymed, heavily alliterative, and rich in laments built on apostrophes, rhetorical questions, and exclamations. To us it seems stiff and foolish, even in the hands of, say, George Gascoigne, who was educated at Cambridge, and who wrote some lyric and satiric verse of considerable merit. Here is a passage from Gascoigne's tragedy *Jocasta,* produced at Gray's Inn in 1566:

Antigone. O doleful day, wherein my sorry sire
    Was born, and yet O more unhappy hour
    When he was crownèd king of stately Thebes.
    The Hymenei, in unhappy bed
    And wicked wedlock, wittingly did join
    The guiltless mother with her guilty son,
    Out of which root we be the branches born
    To bear the scourge of their so foul offense.

If a passage with less narrative content is wanted, the following will do to show the tragic lament full-blown:

Antigone. O weary life, why bid'st thou in my breast
    And I contented be that these mine eyes
    Should see her die that gave to me this life,

And I not 'venge her death by loss of life?
Who can me give a fountain made of moan,
That I may weep as much as is my will,
To souse this sorrow up in swelling tears?

Finally:

Oedipus. O wife, O mother, O both woeful names,
　O woeful mother, and O woeful wife,
　O would to God, alas, O would to God
　Thou ne'er had been my mother, nor my wife.

That Gascoigne is translating does not obscure the kind
or the quality of his verse. Shakespeare must have been
very familiar with this sort of writing; in *A Midsummer
Night's Dream* he neatly parodies (through Bottom's
speech) the lament of the previous generation:

> But stay, O spite!
> But mark, poor knight,
> What dreadful dole is here!
> Eyes, do you see?
> How can it be?
> O dainty duck! O dear!
> Thy mantle good,
> What, stained with blood!
> Approach, ye Furies fell!
> O Fates, come, come,
> Cut thread and thrum;
> Quail, crush, conclude, and quell!
>
> (V.i.268–79)

More subtle, Hotspur's dying words in *1 Henry IV*
have a touch of the same absurd apostrophe and alliteration that marked the older drama and that are appropriate to this anachronistic young knight:

O Harry, thou hast robbed me of my youth!
I better brook the loss of brittle life
Than those proud titles thou hast won of me.

> They wound my thoughts worse than thy sword my flesh.
> But thoughts, the slaves of life, and life, Time's fool. . . .
>
> (V.iv.80–84)

In *Titus* there is a good deal of alliteration, balance, and parallelism, especially in the first two acts:

> Patient yourself, madam, and pardon me
>
> (I.i.121)

> Rome's readiest champions, repose you here in rest
>
> (I.i.151)

> Clear up, fair Queen, that cloudy countenance.
> Though chance of war hath wrought this change of cheer
>
> (I.i.263–64)

> And curtained with a counsel-keeping cave
>
> (II.iii.24)

On the whole the impression is not that of naïveté; or if there is a suggestion of naïveté, it is that of a highly talented writer infatuated with his medium and occasionally forgetful of the dramatic ends that every speech ought to serve. Despite the abundant (almost comically frequent) horrors, the atmosphere is more that of the hothouse than the slaughterhouse; the horrors exist in elegant luxuriance, and though the groundlings probably were delighted, the author must have felt he was creating a drama that would appeal also to the cultivated, who knew Seneca and Ovid.

The Latin quotations that dot the play are the most apparent sign of the lamp, but the fifty-odd mythological allusions are scarcely less apparent. Despite the classical setting, Shakespeare did not have to strew his play with references to Pyramus, Vulcan, Cerberus, Prometheus, Hecuba, the Styx, Dido and Aeneas, Priam, Virginius, and a host of others. *Julius Caesar* has only a tenth as many mythological allusions, but when he wrote *Titus,* Shakespeare evidently was aiming at something quite different from the spare style he was to use in *Julius Caesar.*

In *Titus* he seeks to capture grandeur by abundance. Here is a sample:

> Now climbeth Tamora Olympus' top,
> Safe out of fortune's shot, and sits aloft,
> Secure of thunder's crack or lightning flash,
> Advanced above pale envy's threat'ning reach.
> As when the golden sun salutes the morn,
> And having gilt the ocean with his beams,
> Gallops the zodiac in his glistering coach,
> And overlooks the highest-peering hills;
> So Tamora:
> Upon her wit doth earthly honor wait,
> And virtue stoops and trembles at her frown.
>
> (II.i.1–11)

The simile beginning in line 5 is markedly introduced by the prominent position that "As" occupies in the line, and it is markedly concluded by the similarly prominent "So" in line 9; the explicit allusion to Olympus and the only barely less explicit allusion to Phoebus suggest that Shakespeare is attempting to climb, in Sidney's phrase, to "the height of Seneca his style." (Before the speech is over there will be a reference to Prometheus, and another to Semiramis.) Sidney was speaking, about 1585, of *Gorboduc* (1562), but his words apply to the infinitely superior *Titus:* "it is full of stately speeches and well-sounding phrases."

This heightened style, as well as the conception of a tragic hero pushed beyond the limits of endurance, surely owes something to Seneca, but Ovid, too, helped shape *Titus*. The grisly business of cooking Chiron and Demetrius and serving them as a meat pie to a parent is Ovidian as well as Senecan; Seneca's *Thyestes* includes such a feast, but so too does Ovid's tale of Procne in *Metamorphoses*. In a sense, the stories are inseparable; in *Thyestes,* Atreus himself compares the feast to that in the legend of Procne, and the basic idea of a parent dining on the flesh of his offspring (a vestige of rituals in which the father killed his son as his son became a competitor?)

exists in various myths. In *Titus,* Shakespeare quotes—
rather misquotes—bits of Seneca, but he alludes directly
not only to the legend of Procne but to its rendition in
the *Metamorphoses.* The strong Ovidian influence on
Shakespeare's early writing, especially on the narrative
poems, is beyond all doubt; Francis Meres said in 1598
what must have seemed commonplace: "The sweet witty
soul of Ovid lives in mellifluous and honey-tongued Shakespeare; witness his *Venus and Adonis,* his *Lucrece,* his
sugared sonnets." In *Love's Labor's Lost* a pedant, Holofernes, speaks of Ovid, and though Holofernes can
scarcely be regarded as a reliable mouthpiece, here he
seems to be voicing Shakespeare's opinion, though perhaps a little bumptiously: "For the elegancy, facility, and
golden cadence of poesy, . . . Ovidius Naso was the man"
(IV.ii.127).

Ovid's elegancy, facility, and golden cadence had been
famous even in antiquity (Quintilian said Ovid was unable
to curb his luxuriance—even as Ben Jonson was later to
say that Shakespeare "flowed with that facility that sometime it was necessary he should be stopped"), and to
English playwrights in the latter part of the sixteenth
century Ovid must have seemed with Seneca to be the
man to add dignity to the blatant huffings of earlier
English tragedy. The earlier tragedies with their abundant
"O's" were notably direct; Ovid is often equally direct,
but he is also rich in comparisons. Philomela's severed
tongue "writhed convulsively," a recent translation says,
"like a snake's tail when it has been newly cut off and,
dying, tried to reach its mistress' feet." In Arthur Golding's version of Ovid, which Shakespeare surely knew,
the passage runs thus:

> And with a pair of pinsons fast did catch her by the
> tongue,
> And with his sword did cut it off. The stump whereon
> it hung
> Did patter still. The tip fell down, and quivering on the
> ground
> As though that it had murmured it made a certain sound,

And as an adder's tail cut off doth skip a while, even so
The tip of Philomela's tongue did wriggle to and fro,
And nearer to her mistressward in dying still did go.

Here is Ovid's description (in Golding's words) of
Pyramus' wound: Pyramus drew

His sword, the which among his guts he thrust, and by
   and by
Did draw it from the bleeding wound beginning for to
   die,
And cast himself upon his back. The blood did spin
   on high
As when a conduit pipe is cracked, the water bursting
   out
Doth shoot itself a great way off and pierce the air about.

Probably Shakespeare felt that his description of the
mutilated Lavinia was in the best Ovidian manner:

> Why dost not speak to me?
> Alas, a crimson river of warm blood,
> Like to a bubbling fountain stirred with wind,
> Doth rise and fall between thy rosèd lips,
> Coming and going with thy honey breath.
>
> (II.iv.21–25)

In *Lucrece,* probably written in 1593, within three or four
years of *Titus* and possibly within the same year, Shakespeare wrote:

> And from the purple fountain Brutus drew
>   The murd'rous knife, and, as it left the place,
>   Her blood, in poor revenge, held it in chase.
>
> (1734–36)

To defend *Lucrece* would be even more difficult than to
defend *Titus,* but it ought to be evident that Shakespeare
is attempting to make art out of violence. For naked violence we must turn, say, to *Lear,* where a woman plucks

an old man's beard, urges her husband to gouge out the old man's eyes, and stabs a servant in the back. In *Titus* the horror is for the most part elevated, or at least veiled by ingenuity.

This is not to say that Shakespeare's treatment of horror is successful in *Titus:* the testimony of generations of readers (few playgoers have had the chance to see *Titus*) strongly suggests that it is unsuccessful. The elaborate treatment occasionally disgusts us, though perhaps it was meant to distance the horror and thereby make it acceptable. But in its day, and for a couple of decades after, the play was popular; as late as 1614 Ben Jonson grumbled that *Titus* still had its admirers. It is a remarkable achievement, superior in character, in plot, and in language to *The Spanish Tragedy,* and it rivals Marlowe, whose plays are the only other major plays of the period. Its exuberance, though in places distressing, is a sign of imaginative fertility that was later to be splendidly husbanded. It is, of course, a play that is of its age, but if we strongly have this impression, is it not partly because Shakespeare went on to write plays that are not of an age but for all time?

SYLVAN BARNET

The Most Lamentable Roman Tragedy
of
Titus Andronicus

[Dramatis Personae

Saturninus, son to the late Emperor of Rome,
    afterward Emperor
Bassianus, brother to Saturninus
Titus Andronicus, a noble Roman
Marcus Andronicus, Tribune, and brother to Titus
Lucius ⎱
Quintus ⎰
Martius ⎰   sons to Titus Andronicus
Mutius ⎰
Young Lucius, a boy, son to Lucius
Publius, son to Marcus Andronicus
Sempronius ⎱
Caius ⎰   kinsmen to Titus Andronicus
Valentine ⎰
Aemilius, a noble Roman
Alarbus ⎱
Demetrius ⎰ sons to Tamora
Chiron ⎰
Aaron, a Moor, beloved by Tamora
A Captain
A Messenger
A Clown
Tamora, Queen of the Goths
Lavinia, daughter to Titus Andronicus
Nurse, and a blackamoor Infant
Romans, Goths, Senators, Tribunes, Officers,
    Soldiers, and Attendants

Scene: Rome, and the countryside near it]

The Most Lamentable Roman Tragedy
of Titus Andronicus

[ACT I

Scene I. *Rome. Before the Capitol.*]

*[Flourish.°1] Enter the Tribunes and Senators
aloft; and then enter Saturninus and his followers
at one door, and Bassianus and his followers [at
the other,] with drums and trumpets.*

Saturninus. Noble patricians, patrons of my right,
  Defend the justice of my cause with arms;
  And, countrymen, my loving followers,
  Plead my successive title° with your swords.
  I am his first-born son that was the last   5
  That ware the imperial diadem of Rome;
  Then let my father's honors live in me,
  Nor wrong mine age° with this indignity.

Bassianus. Romans, friends, followers, favorers of my
      right,
  If ever Bassianus, Caesar's son,   10

---

1 The degree sign (°) indicates a footnote, which is keyed to the
text by line number. Text references are printed in *italic* type; the
annotation follows in roman type. I.i.s.d. *Flourish* trumpet fanfare
4 *successive title* right to the succession   8 *age* i.e., seniority

Were gracious° in the eyes of royal Rome,
Keep° then this passage to the Capitol,
And suffer not dishonor to approach
The imperial seat, to virtue consecrate,
To justice, continence,° and nobility;
But let desert in pure election shine,
And, Romans, fight for freedom in your choice.

Marcus. (*With the crown*) Princes, that strive by fac-
    tions and by friends
Ambitiously for rule and empery,°
Know that the people of Rome, for whom we stand
A special party, have by common voice,
In election for the Roman empery,
Chosen Andronicus, surnamèd Pius
For many good and great deserts to Rome.
A nobler man, a braver warrior,
Lives not this day within the city walls.
He by the senate is accited° home
From weary wars against the barbarous Goths;
That with his sons, a terror to our foes,
Hath yoked° a nation strong, trained up in arms.
Ten years are spent since first he undertook
This cause of Rome, and chastisèd with arms
Our enemies' pride: five times he hath returned
Bleeding to Rome, bearing his valiant sons
In coffins from the field.°
And now at last, laden with honor's spoils,
Returns the good Andronicus to Rome,
Renownèd Titus, flourishing in arms.
Let us entreat, by honor of his name,
Whom worthily you would have now succeed,

11 *gracious* acceptable   12 *Keep* guard   15 *continence* restraint
19 *empery* dominion (but in line 22 *empery* = emperor)   27 *accited*
summoned   30 *yoked* subjugated   35 *field* (this word is followed
by: "and at this day/To the monument of that Andronici/Done
sacrifice of expiation,/And slain the noblest prisoner of the Goths."
These lines, omitted from the second and third quartos and from
the Folio, are inconsistent with the ensuing action, in which Alarbus
is sacrificed. Perhaps Shakespeare neglected to cancel them in the
manuscript after deciding to make Alarbus' execution part of the
action)

And in the Capitol and Senate's right,°
Whom you pretend° to honor and adore,
That you withdraw you and abate your strength,
Dismiss your followers, and, as suitors should,
Plead your deserts in peace and humbleness.   45

Saturninus. How fair° the tribune speaks to calm my
    thoughts!

Bassianus. Marcus Andronicus, so I do affy°
In thy uprightness and integrity,
And so I love and honor thee and thine,
Thy noble brother Titus and his sons,   50
And her to whom my thoughts are humbled all,
Gracious Lavinia, Rome's rich ornament,
That I will here dismiss my loving friends;
And to my fortunes and the people's favor
Commit my cause in balance to be weighed.   55
                              Exit [*his*] *soldiers.*

Saturninus. Friends, that have been thus forward in
    my right,
I thank you all, and here dismiss you all,
And to the love and favor of my country
Commit myself, my person, and the cause.°
                       [*Exeunt his followers.*]
Rome, be as just and gracious unto me   60
As I am confident and kind° to thee.
Open the gates and let me in.

Bassianus. Tribunes, and me, a poor competitor.°
    [*Flourish.*] *They go up into the Senate house.*

            Enter a Captain.

Captain. Romans, make way! The good Andronicus,
Patron° of virtue, Rome's best champion,   65
Successful in the battles that he fights,
With honor and with fortune is returned
From where he circumscribèd with his sword

41 *the Capitol and Senate's right* the right of the Capitol and the
Senate   42 *pretend* claim   46 *fair* courteously   47 *affy* trust   59
cause affair   61 *confident and kind* trusting and natural(ly devoted)
63 *competitor* candidate   65 *Patron* representative

And brought to yoke the enemies of Rome.

Sound drums and trumpets, and then enter two of Titus' sons, and then two men bearing a coffin covered with black, then two other sons, then Titus Andronicus, and then Tamora, the Queen of Goths, and her three sons, [Alarbus,] Chiron, and Demetrius, with Aaron the Moor, and others as many as can be; then set down the coffin, and Titus speaks.

70 *Titus.* Hail, Rome, victorious in thy mourning weeds!°
Lo, as the bark that hath discharged his fraught°
Returns with precious lading to the bay
From whence at first she weighed her anchorage,°
Cometh Andronicus, bound with laurel boughs,
75 To re-salute his country with his tears,
Tears of true joy for his return to Rome.
Thou° great defender of this Capitol,
Stand gracious to the rites that we intend!
Romans, of five and twenty valiant sons,
80 Half of the number that King Priam had,
Behold the poor remains, alive and dead!
These that survive let Rome reward with love;
These that I bring unto their latest° home,
With burial amongst their ancestors.
Here Goths have given me leave to sheathe my
85   sword.
Titus, unkind° and careless of thine own,
Why suffer'st thou thy sons, unburied yet,
To hover on the dreadful shore of Styx?°
Make way to lay them by their brethren.°
                    They open the tomb.
90 There greet in silence, as the dead are wont,
And sleep in peace, slain in your country's wars!
O sacred receptacle of my joys,
Sweet cell of virtue and nobility,

70 *weeds* apparel   71 *his fraught* its freight   73 *anchorage* anchors
77 *Thou* i.e., Jupiter   83 *latest* last   86 *unkind* unnatural   88 *Styx*
river surrounding Hades   89 *brethren* (trisyllabic here and occasionally elsewhere: "breth-e-rin")

How many sons hast thou of mine in store,
That thou wilt never render to me more!   95

Lucius. Give us the proudest prisoner of the Goths,
That we may hew his limbs, and on a pile
Ad manes fratrum° sacrifice his flesh,
Before this earthy prison of their bones,
That so the shadows be not unappeased,   100
Nor we disturbed with prodigies° on earth.

Titus. I give him you, the noblest that survives,
The eldest son of this distressèd queen.

Tamora. Stay, Roman brethren! Gracious conqueror,   105
Victorious Titus, rue the tears I shed,
A mother's tears in passion° for her son:
And if thy sons were ever dear to thee,
O, think my son to be as dear to me!
Sufficeth not that we are brought to Rome,
To beautify thy triumphs° and return,   110
Captive to thee and to thy Roman yoke,
But must my sons be slaughtered in the streets,
For valiant doings in their country's cause?
O, if to fight for king and commonweal
Were piety in thine, it is in these.   115
Andronicus, stain not thy tomb with blood.
Wilt thou draw near the nature of the gods?
Draw near them then in being merciful;
Sweet mercy is nobility's true badge.
Thrice-noble Titus, spare my first-born son.   120

Titus. Patient° yourself, madam, and pardon me.
These are their brethren, whom your Goths beheld
Alive and dead, and for their brethren slain
Religiously they ask a sacrifice.
To this your son is marked, and die he must,   125
T' appease their groaning shadows that are gone.

Lucius. Away with him! And make a fire straight,

---

98 *Ad manes fratrum* to the ghosts of our brothers (Latin)
101 *prodigies* ominous disturbances   106 *passion* violent emotion
110 *triumphs* triumphal processions   121 *Patient* calm

And with our swords, upon a pile of wood,
Let's hew his limbs till they be clean consumed.
Exit Titus' sons with Alarbus.

130 *Tamora.* O cruel, irreligious piety!

Chiron. Was never Scythia° half so barbarous.

Demetrius. Oppose° not Scythia to ambitious Rome.
    Alarbus goes to rest, and we survive
    To tremble under Titus' threat'ning look.
135 Then, madam, stand resolved, but hope withal°
    The selfsame gods that armed the Queen of Troy°
    With opportunity of sharp revenge
    Upon the Thracian tyrant in his tent
    May favor Tamora, the Queen of Goths,
140 (When Goths were Goths and Tamora was queen)
    To quit° the bloody wrongs upon her foes.

Enter the sons of Andronicus again.

Lucius. See, lord and father, how we have performed
    Our Roman rites! Alarbus' limbs are lopped,
    And entrails feed the sacrificing fire,
145 Whose smoke like incense doth perfume the sky.
    Remaineth naught but to inter our brethren,
    And with loud 'larums° welcome them to Rome.

Titus. Let it be so, and let Andronicus
    Make this his latest farewell to their souls.
                *Sound trumpets, and lay the coffin
                in the tomb.*

150 In peace and honor rest you here, my sons,
    Rome's readiest champions, repose you here in rest,
    Secure from worldly chances and mishaps!
    Here lurks no treason, here no envy° swells,
    Here grow no damnèd drugs,° here are no storms,

---

131 *Scythia* a region in southern Russia noted for its savage inhabitants 132 *Oppose* compare 135 *withal* with this 136 *Queen of Troy* Hecuba (who murdered the sons of Polymnestor—*the Thracian tyrant* of line 138—in revenge for his murder of her son) 141 *quit* requite, repay 147 *'larums* alarums, calls to arms 153 *envy* malice 154 *drugs* poisonous plants

No noise, but silence and eternal sleep: *155*
In peace and honor rest you here, my sons!

Enter Lavinia.

Lavinia. In peace and honor live Lord Titus long,
My noble lord and father, live in fame!
Lo, at this tomb my tributary° tears
I render for my brethren's obsequies, *160*
And at thy feet I kneel, with tears of joy
Shed on this earth for thy return to Rome.
O, bless me here with thy victorious hand,
Whose fortunes Rome's best citizens applaud.

Titus. Kind Rome, that hast thus lovingly reserved *165*
The cordial° of mine age to glad my heart!
Lavinia, live, outlive thy father's days
And fame's eternal date,° for virtue's praise!

[*Enter above Marcus Andronicus, Saturninus,
Bassianus, and others.*]

Marcus. Long live Lord Titus, my belovèd brother,
Gracious triumpher in the eyes of Rome! *170*

Titus. Thanks, gentle tribune, noble brother Marcus.

Marcus. And welcome, nephews, from successful wars,
You that survive, and you that sleep in fame!
Fair lords, your fortunes are alike in all,
That in your country's service drew your swords, *175*
But safer triumph is this funeral pomp,
That hath aspired° to Solon's happiness°
And triumphs over chance in honor's bed.
Titus Andronicus, the people of Rome,
Whose friend in justice thou hast ever been, *180*
Send thee by me, their tribune and their trust,
This palliament° of white and spotless hue,
And name thee in election for the empire
With these our late-deceasèd emperor's sons:

159 *tributary* given as tribute 166 *cordial* comfort (literally: stimulant to the heart) 168 *date* duration 177 *aspired* risen 177 *Solon's happiness* (Solon said: "Call no man happy until he is dead") 182 *palliament* robe

185   Be *candidatus*° then, and put it on,
          And help to set a head on headless Rome.

      Titus. A better head her glorious body fits
          Than his that shakes for age and feebleness:
          What° should I don this robe and trouble you?
190   Be chosen with proclamations today,
          Tomorrow yield up rule, resign my life,
          And set abroad new business for you all?
          Rome, I have been thy soldier forty years,
          And led my country's strength successfully,
195   And buried one and twenty valiant sons,
          Knighted in field, slain manfully in arms,
          In right and service of their noble country:
          Give me a staff of honor for mine age,
          But not a scepter to control the world.
200   Upright he held it, lords, that held it last.

      Marcus. Titus, thou shalt obtain and ask° the empery.

      Saturninus. Proud and ambitious tribune, canst thou
         tell?

      Titus. Patience, Prince Saturninus.

      Saturninus.   Romans, do me right.
          Patricians, draw your swords and sheathe them not
205   Till Saturninus be Rome's emperor.
          Andronicus, would thou were shipped to hell
          Rather than rob me of the people's hearts.

      Lucius. Proud Saturnine, interrupter of the good
          That noble-minded Titus means to thee!

210   *Titus.* Content thee, Prince, I will restore to thee
          The people's hearts, and wean them from them-
          selves.

      Bassianus. Andronicus, I do not flatter thee,
          But honor thee, and will do till I die.
          My faction if thou strengthen with thy friends,

185 *candidatus* candidate (Latin; literally: clad in white)   189
What why   201 *obtain and ask* i.e., obtain if you ask for

I will most thankful be, and thanks to men   215
Of noble minds is honorable meed.°

Titus. People of Rome, and people's tribunes here,
I ask your voices and your suffrages:
Will ye bestow them friendly on Andronicus?

Tribunes. To gratify the good Andronicus,   220
And gratulate° his safe return to Rome,
The people will accept whom he admits.°

Titus. Tribunes, I thank you, and this suit I make,
That you create our emperor's eldest son,
Lord Saturnine; whose virtues will, I hope,   225
Reflect on Rome as Titan's° rays on earth,
And ripen justice in this commonweal:
Then, if you will elect by my advice,
Crown him and say, "Long live our emperor!"

Marcus. With voices and applause of every sort,   230
Patricians and plebeians, we create
Lord Saturninus Rome's great emperor,
And say "Long live our Emperor Saturnine!"
            [*A long flourish till they come down.*]

Saturninus. Titus Andronicus, for thy favors done
To us in our election° this day,   235
I give thee thanks in° part of thy deserts,
And will with deeds requite thy gentleness:°
And for an onset,° Titus, to advance
Thy name and honorable family,
Lavinia will I make my empress,°   240
Rome's royal mistress, mistress of my heart,
And in the sacred Pantheon° her espouse.
Tell me, Andronicus, doth this motion° please thee?

Titus. It doth, my worthy lord, and in this match

216 *meed* reward   221 *gratulate* rejoice at   222 *admits* approves
226 *Titan's* the sun god's   235 *election* (here, as often in Shakespeare, *-ion* is disyllabic)   236 *in* as   237 *gentleness* nobility
238 *onset* beginning   240 *empress* (here, and often elsewhere in
Titus, trisyllabic: "em-per-es")   242 *Pantheon* temple dedicated to
all the gods   243 *motion* proposal

245   I hold me highly honored of your grace,
And here in sight of Rome to Saturnine,
King and commander of our commonweal,
The wide world's emperor, do I consecrate
My sword, my chariot, and my prisoners,
250   Presents well worthy Rome's imperious° lord.
Receive them then, the tribute that I owe,
Mine honor's ensigns° humbled at thy feet.

Saturninus. Thanks, noble Titus, father of my life!
How proud I am of thee and of thy gifts
255   Rome shall record, and when I do forget
The least of these unspeakable deserts,
Romans, forget your fealty° to me.

Titus. [*To Tamora*] Now, madam, are you prisoner to
an emperor,
To him that, for your honor and your state,
260   Will use you nobly and your followers.

Saturninus. [*Aside*] A goodly lady, trust me, of the
hue
That I would choose, were I to choose anew.
[*Aloud*] Clear up, fair Queen, that cloudy coun-
tenance.
Though chance of war hath wrought this change
of cheer,°
265   Thou com'st not to be made a scorn in Rome.
Princely shall be thy usage every way.
Rest on my word, and let not discontent
Daunt all your hopes. Madam, he° comforts you
Can make you greater than the Queen of Goths.
270   Lavinia, you are not displeased with this?

Lavinia. Not I, my lord, sith° true nobility
Warrants° these words in princely courtesy.

Saturninus. Thanks, sweet Lavinia. Romans, let us go.

---

250 *imperious* imperial   252 *ensigns* tokens   257 *fealty* loyalty
264 *cheer* countenance   268 *he* he who   271 *sith* since   272 *Warrants* justifies

Ransomless here we set our prisoners free.
Proclaim our honors, lords, with trump and drum. *275*

Bassianus. Lord Titus, by your leave, this maid is
mine.

Titus. How, sir! Are you in earnest then, my lord?

Bassianus. Ay, noble Titus, and resolved withal
To do myself this reason and this right.

Marcus. Suum cuique° is our Roman justice. *280*
This prince in justice seizeth but his own.

Lucius. And that he will, and shall, if Lucius live.

Titus. Traitors, avaunt!° Where is the Emperor's
guard?
Treason, my lord! Lavinia is surprised!°

Saturninus. Surprised! By whom?

Bassianus.   By him that justly may *285*
Bear his betrothed from all the world away.
[*Exeunt Marcus and Bassianus, with Lavinia.*]

Mutius. Brothers, help to convey her hence away,
And with my sword I'll keep this door° safe.
[*Exeunt Lucius, Quintus, and Martius.*]

Titus. Follow, my lord, and I'll soon bring her back.
[*During the fray, exeunt Saturninus, Tamora,
Demetrius, Chiron, and Aaron.*]

Mutius. My lord, you pass not here. *290*

Titus. What, villain boy! Barr'st me my way in Rome?
[*He stabs Mutius.*]

Mutius. [*Dying*] Help, Lucius, help!

[*Enter Lucius.*]

Lucius. My lord, you are unjust; and more than so,

---

280 *Suum cuique* to each his own (Latin) 283 *avaunt* be gone
284 *surprised* suddenly taken 288 *door* (disyllabic)

    In wrongful quarrel you have slain your son.

295 *Titus.* Nor thou, nor he, are any sons of mine:
    My sons would never so dishonor me.
    Traitor, restore Lavinia to the Emperor.

    Lucius. Dead if you will, but not to be his wife
    That is another's lawful promised love.   [*Exit.*]

    *Enter aloft the Emperor with Tamora and her
    two sons and Aaron the Moor.*

300 *Saturninus.* No, Titus, no; the Emperor needs her not,
    Nor her, nor thee, nor any of thy stock:
    I'll trust by leisure° him that mocks me once;
    Thee never, nor thy traitorous haughty sons,
    Confederates all thus to dishonor me.
305   Was none in Rome to make a stale°
    But Saturnine? Full well, Andronicus,
    Agree these deeds with that proud brag of thine,
    That saidst I begged the empire at thy hands.

    Titus. O monstrous! What reproachful words are
    these?

    Saturninus. But go thy ways, go, give that changing
310   piece°
    To him that flourished for her with his sword:
    A valiant son-in-law thou shalt enjoy,
    One fit to bandy° with thy lawless sons,
    To ruffle° in the commonwealth of Rome.

315 *Titus.* These words are razors to my wounded heart.

    Saturninus. And therefore, lovely Tamora, Queen of
    Goths,
    That like the stately Phoebe° 'mongst her nymphs
    Dost overshine the gallant'st dames of Rome,
    If thou be pleased with this my sudden choice,
320   Behold, I choose thee, Tamora, for my bride,

302 *by leisure* slowly   305 *stale* laughingstock   310 *changing piece*
fickle wench   313 *bandy* contend, bicker   314 *ruffle* brawl   317
Phoebe Diana, goddess of the moon

And will create thee Empress of Rome.
Speak, Queen of Goths, dost thou applaud my
   choice?
And here I swear by all the Roman gods,
Sith priest and holy water are so near,
And tapers burn so bright, and everything   *325*
In readiness for Hymenaeus° stand,
I will not re-salute the streets of Rome,
Or climb my palace, till from forth this place
I lead espoused my bride along with me.

Tamora. And here in sight of heaven to Rome I
   swear,
If Saturnine advance the Queen of Goths,   *330*
She will a handmaid be to his desires,
A loving nurse, a mother to his youth.

Saturninus. Ascend, fair Queen, Pantheon. Lords, ac-
   company
Your noble emperor and his lovely bride,
Sent by the heavens for Prince Saturnine,   *335*
Whose wisdom hath her fortune conquerèd.
There shall we consummate our spousal rites.
             Exeunt omnes° [except Titus].

Titus. I am not bid° to wait upon this bride.
Titus, when wert thou wont to walk alone,   *340*
Dishonored thus and challengèd° of wrongs?

     Enter Marcus and Titus' sons [Lucius,
         Quintus, and Martius].

Marcus. O Titus, see, O, see, what thou hast done!
In a bad quarrel slain a virtuous son.

Titus. No, foolish tribune, no; no son of mine,
Nor thou, nor these, confederates in the deed   *345*
That hath dishonored all our family,
Unworthy brother, and unworthy sons!

326 *Hymenaeus* god of marriage   338 s.d. *omnes* all (Latin)   339
bid asked   341 *challengèd* accused

Lucius. But let us give him burial as becomes;°
    Give Mutius burial with our brethren.

350 *Titus.* Traitors, away! He rests not in this tomb:
    This monument five hundred years hath stood,
    Which I have sumptuously re-edified:°
    Here none but soldiers and Rome's servitors
    Repose in fame; none basely slain in brawls.
355   Bury him where you can, he comes not here.

Marcus. My lord, this is impiety in you.
    My nephew Mutius' deeds do plead for him;
    He must be buried with his brethren.

       Titus' two sons speak:

[*Quintus, Martius.*] And shall, or him we will accompany.

360 *Titus.* And shall? What villain was it spake that word?

       Titus' son speaks.

[*Quintus.*] He that would vouch it in any place but
    here.

Titus. What, would you bury him in my despite?°

Marcus. No, noble Titus, but entreat of thee
    To pardon Mutius and to bury him.

365 *Titus.* Marcus, even thou hast stroke upon my crest,
    And with these boys mine honor thou hast wounded.
    My foes I do repute° you every one,
    So trouble me no more, but get you gone.

Martius. He is not with himself; let us withdraw.

370 *Quintus.* Not I, till Mutius' bones be buried.
            The brother and the sons kneel.

Marcus. Brother, for in that name doth nature plead—

Quintus. Father, and in that name doth nature speak—

---

348 *becomes* is fitting   352 *re-edified* rebuilt   362 *in my despite* in
spite of me   367 *repute* consider

Titus. Speak thou no more, if all the rest will speed.°

Marcus. Renownèd Titus, more than half my soul—

Lucius. Dear father, soul and substance of us all—   375

Marcus. Suffer° thy brother Marcus to inter
His noble nephew here in virtue's nest,
That died in honor and Lavinia's cause.
Thou art a Roman, be not barbarous:
The Greeks upon advice° did bury Ajax°   380
That slew himself; and wise Laertes' son°
Did graciously plead for his funerals:
Let not young Mutius then, that was thy joy,
Be barred his entrance here.

Titus.   Rise, Marcus, rise.
The dismal'st day is this that e'er I saw,   385
To be dishonored by my sons in Rome!
Well, bury him, and bury me the next.

                    They put him in the tomb.

Lucius. There lie thy bones, sweet Mutius, with thy
    friends,
Till we with trophies do adorn thy tomb.

          They all kneel and say:

[*All.*] No man shed tears for noble Mutius,   390
He lives in fame that died in virtue's cause.

Marcus. My lord, to step out of these dreary dumps,°
How comes it that the subtle Queen of Goths
Is of a sudden thus advanced in Rome?

Titus. I know not, Marcus, but I know it is;   395
(Whether° by device° or no, the heavens can tell.)
Is she not then beholding° to the man
That brought her for this high good turn so far?
Yes, and will nobly him remunerate.

373 *if all the rest will speed* if the rest is to go well (?) if the rest of
you wish to live (?)   376 *Suffer* allow   380 *advice* deliberation
380 *Ajax* (when Achilles' arms were given to Odysseus, Ajax in a
fury stabbed himself)   381 *Laertes' son* Odysseus   392 *dumps* blues,
melancholy state   396 *Whether* (probably pronounced "where")
396 *device* plot   397 *beholding* beholden, indebted

*Enter the Emperor, Tamora and her two sons, with
the Moor at one door. Enter at the other door
Bassianus and Lavinia, with others.*

400 *Saturninus.* So Bassianus, you have played your prize:°
      God give you joy, sir, of your gallant bride!

Bassianus. And you of yours, my lord! I say no more,
      Nor wish no less, and so I take my leave.

Saturninus. Traitor, if Rome have law, or we have
      power,
405   Thou and thy faction shall repent this rape.

Bassianus. Rape, call you it, my lord, to seize my own,
      My true-betrothèd love, and now my wife?
      But let the laws of Rome determine all;
      Meanwhile am I possessed of that is mine.

410 *Saturninus.* 'Tis good, sir; you are very short with us,
      But if we live we'll be as sharp with you.

Bassianus. My lord, what I have done, as best I may
      Answer I must, and shall do with my life.
      Only thus much I give your grace to know—
415   By all the duties that I owe to Rome,
      This noble gentleman, Lord Titus here,
      Is in opinion° and in honor wronged,
      That, in the rescue of Lavinia,
      With his own hand did slay his youngest son,
420   In zeal to you, and highly moved to wrath
      To be controlled° in that he frankly° gave.
      Receive him then to favor, Saturnine,
      That hath expressed himself in all his deeds
      A father and a friend to thee and Rome.

425 *Titus.* Prince Bassianus, leave to plead° my deeds;
      'Tis thou and those that have dishonored me.
      Rome and the righteous heavens be my judge,
      How I have loved and honored Saturnine!

---

400 *played your prize* won your contest   417 *opinion* reputation
421 *controlled* opposed   421 *frankly* generously   425 *leave to
plead* cease pleading

Tamora. My worthy lord, if ever Tamora
    Were gracious in those princely eyes of thine,   *430*
    Then hear me speak indifferently° for all;
    And at my suit, sweet, pardon what is past.

Saturninus. What, madam! Be dishonored openly,
    And basely put it up° without revenge?

Tamora. Not so, my lord, the gods of Rome forfend°   *435*
    I should be author° to dishonor you!
    But on mine honor dare I undertake°
    For good Lord Titus' innocence in all,
    Whose fury not dissembled speaks his griefs:
    Then at my suit look graciously on him;
    Lose not so noble a friend on vain suppose,°   *440*
    Nor with sour looks afflict his gentle heart.
    [*Aside*] My lord, be ruled by me, be won at last,
    Dissemble all your griefs and discontents—
    You are but newly planted in your throne—
    Lest then the people, and patricians too,   *445*
    Upon a just survey, take Titus' part,
    And so supplant you for ingratitude,
    Which Rome reputes to be a heinous sin.
    Yield at entreats:° and then let me alone.°   *450*
    I'll find a day to massacre them all,
    And race° their faction and their family,
    The cruel father and his traitorous sons,
    To whom I suèd for my dear son's life;
    And make them know what 'tis to let a queen   *455*
    Kneel in the streets and beg for grace in vain.
    [*Aloud*] Come, come, sweet Emperor—come, An-
        dronicus—
    Take up this good old man, and cheer the heart
    That dies in tempest of thy angry frown.

Saturninus. Rise, Titus, rise, my empress hath pre-
      vailed.   *460*

431 *indifferently* impartially   434 *put it up* (the figure is of putting
up, or sheathing, a sword)   435 *forfend* forbid   436 *author* agent
437 *undertake* assert   441 *vain suppose* empty supposition   450 *at
entreats* to entreaties   450 *let me alone* i.e., leave it to me   452 *race*
root out

Titus. I thank your Majesty, and her, my lord.
These words, these looks, infuse new life in me.

Tamora. Titus, I am incorporate in Rome,
A Roman now adopted happily,
465   And must advise the Emperor for his good.
This day all quarrels die, Andronicus.
And let it be mine honor, good my lord,
That I have reconciled your friends and you.
For you, Prince Bassianus, I have passed
470   My word and promise to the Emperor
That you will be more mild and tractable.
And fear not, lords, and you, Lavinia;
By my advice, all humbled on your knees,
You shall ask pardon of his Majesty.

[*Lucius.*] We do, and vow to heaven, and to his high-
475   ness,
That what we did was mildly as we might,°
Tend'ring° our sister's honor and our own.

Marcus. That on mine honor here do I protest.

Saturninus. Away, and talk not, trouble us no more.

Tamora. Nay, nay, sweet Emperor, we must all be
480   friends.
The tribune and his nephews kneel for grace.
I will not be denied. Sweet heart, look back.

Saturninus. Marcus, for thy sake, and thy brother's
       here,
And at my lovely Tamora's entreats,
485   I do remit these young men's heinous faults.
Stand up.
Lavinia, though you left me like a churl,
I found a friend, and sure as death I swore
I would not part° a bachelor from the priest.
490   Come, if the Emperor's court can feast two brides,
You are my guest, Lavinia, and your friends.

476 *mildly as we might* as mild as we might do   477 *Tend'ring*
having regard for   489 *part* depart

This day shall be a love-day,° Tamora.

Titus. Tomorrow, and° it please your Majesty
To hunt the panther and the hart with me,
With horn and hound we'll give your Grace bon-
    jour.°   *495*
Saturninus. Be it so, Titus, and gramercy° too.

                                                    Exeunt.

Sound trumpets. Manet° [*Aaron the*] *Moor.*

492 *love-day* day appointed to settle disputes (with a pun on day
for love)   493 *and* if   495 *bonjour* good morning (French)   496
gramercy thanks   496 s.d. *Manet* remains (Latin. Clearly this and
the next scene are continuous; the Folio's incorrect division into
acts is retained merely to facilitate reference)

[ACT II

Scene I. *Rome. Before the palace.*
Aaron alone.]

Aaron. Now climbeth Tamora Olympus'° top,
  Safe out of fortune's shot, and sits aloft,
  Secure of° thunder's crack or lightning flash,
  Advanced above pale envy's° threat'ning reach.
5 As when the golden sun salutes the morn,
  And having gilt the ocean with his beams,
  Gallops° the zodiac in his glistering coach,
  And overlooks° the highest-peering hills;
  So Tamora:
10 Upon her wit doth earthly honor wait,
  And virtue stoops and trembles at her frown.
  Then, Aaron, arm thy heart, and fit thy thoughts
  To mount aloft with thy imperial mistress,
  And mount her pitch,° whom thou in triumph long
15 Hast prisoner held, fettered in amorous chains,
  And faster bound to Aaron's charming° eyes
  Than is Prometheus° tied to Caucasus.
  Away with slavish weeds° and servile thoughts!
  I will be bright and shine in pearl and gold
20 To wait upon this new-made empress.
  To wait, said I? To wanton with this queen,

II.i.1 *Olympus* Mount Olympus (reputed home of the gods)   3 *of* from   4 *envy's* hate's   7 *Gallops* gallops through   8 *overlooks* looks down upon   14 *mount her pitch* rise to the highest point of her flight (a term from falconry)   16 *charming* spellbinding   17 *Prometheus* a Titan fettered to a rock in the Caucasus because he stole fire from heaven   18 *weeds* apparel

This goddess, this Semiramis,° this nymph,
This siren, that will charm Rome's Saturnine
And see his shipwrack and his commonweal's.
Hollo! What storm is this?   25

Enter Chiron and Demetrius, braving.°

Demetrius. Chiron, thy years wants° wit, thy wits
     wants edge,
And manners, to intrude where I am graced,°
And may for aught thou knowest affected° be.

Chiron. Demetrius, thou dost overween° in all,
And so in this, to bear me down with braves.°   30
'Tis not the difference of a year or two
Makes me less gracious,° or thee more fortunate;
I am as able and as fit as thou
To serve, and to deserve my mistress' grace;
And that my sword upon thee shall approve,°   35
And plead my passions for Lavinia's love.

Aaron. Clubs, clubs!° These lovers will not keep the
     peace.

Demetrius. Why, boy, although our mother, unad-
     vised,°
Gave you a dancing-rapier° by your side,
Are you so desperate grown, to threat your friends?   40
Go to; have your lath° glued within your sheath,
Till you know better how to handle it.

Chiron. Meanwhile, sir, with the little skill I have,
Full well shalt thou perceive how much I dare.
                                                  They draw.

Demetrius. Ay, boy, grow ye so brave?

Aaron.   Why, how now, lords!   45

22 *Semiramis* legendary Assyrian queen, noted for her lust and
beauty   25 s.d. *braving* challenging   26 *wants* (the ending *-s* is
frequently found with a plural subject)   27 *graced* favored   28
affected loved   29 *overween* arrogantly presume   30 *braves* threats
32 *gracious* acceptable   35 *approve* prove   37 *Clubs, clubs* (the
cry raised to call the watch to separate brawlers in London)
38 *unadvised* unwisely   39 *dancing-rapier* ornamental light sword
41 *lath* wooden (stage) sword

So near the Emperor's palace dare ye draw,
And maintain such a quarrel openly?
Full well I wot° the ground of all this grudge.
I would not for a million of gold
50   The cause were known to them it most concerns,
Nor would your noble mother for much more
Be so dishonored in the court of Rome.
For shame, put up.°

Demetrius.   Not I, till I have sheathed
My rapier in his bosom, and withal
55   Thrust those reproachful speeches down his throat,
That he hath breathed in my dishonor here.

Chiron. For that I am prepared and full resolved,
Foul-spoken coward, that thund'rest with thy tongue
And with thy weapon nothing dar'st perform.

60 *Aaron.* Away, I say!
Now, by the gods that warlike Goths adore,
This petty brabble° will undo us all.
Why, lords, and think you not how dangerous
It is to jet° upon a prince's right?
65   What, is Lavinia then become so loose,
Or Bassianus so degenerate,
That for her love such quarrels may be broached
Without controlment, justice, or revenge?
Young lords, beware! And should the Empress know
70   This discord's ground,° the music would not please.

Chiron. I care not, I, knew she and all the world:
I love Lavinia more than all the world.

Demetrius. Youngling, learn thou to make some
     meaner° choice.
Lavinia is thine elder brother's hope.

75 *Aaron.* Why, are ye mad? Or know ye not, in Rome
How furious and impatient they be,

48 *wot* know   53 *put up* sheathe your weapons   62 *brabble* brawl
64 *jet* encroach   70 *ground* reason (with a pun on the musical
meaning: bass to a descant)   73 *meaner* lower

And cannot brook competitors in love?
I tell you, lords, you do but plot your deaths
By this device.

Chiron.   Aaron, a thousand deaths
Would I propose° to achieve her whom I love.   *80*

Aaron. To achieve her how?

Demetrius.   Why makes thou it so strange?°
She is a woman, therefore may be wooed;
She is a woman, therefore may be won;
She is Lavinia, therefore must be loved.
What, man! More water glideth by the mill   *85*
Than wots the miller of, and easy it is
Of a cut loaf to steal a shive,° we know:
Though Bassianus be the Emperor's brother,
Better than he have worn Vulcan's badge.°

Aaron. [*Aside*] Ay, and as good as Saturninus may.   *90*

Demetrius. Then why should he despair that knows
        to court it
With words, fair looks, and liberality?
What, hast not thou full often stroke a doe,
And borne her cleanly by the keeper's nose?

Aaron. Why then, it seems, some certain snatch° or so   *95*
Would serve your turns.

Chiron.   Ay, so the turn were served.

Demetrius. Aaron, thou hast hit it.

Aaron.   Would you had hit it too,
Then should not we be tired with this ado.
Why, hark ye, hark ye! And are you such fools
To square° for this? Would it offend you then   *100*
That both should speed?°

---

80 *propose* be willing to meet   81 *Why makes thou it so strange*
why do you seem surprised   87 *shive* slice   89 *Vulcan's badge* i.e.,
the horns of cuckoldry (Vulcan's wife, Venus, deceived him with
Mars)   95 *snatch* catch (the likelihood that there is also a sexual
meaning here is increased by *turns* in the next line, a word often
denoting sexual acts)   100 *square* quarrel   101 *speed* prosper

Chiron.   Faith, not me.

Demetrius. Nor me, so I were one.

Aaron. For shame, be friends, and join for that you
       jar.°
       'Tis policy° and stratagem must do
105 That you affect,° and so must you resolve,
       That what you cannot as you would achieve,
       You must perforce° accomplish as you may.
       Take this of me, Lucrece° was not more chaste
       Than this Lavinia, Bassianus' love.
110 A speedier course than ling'ring languishment
       Must we pursue, and I have found the path.
       My lords, a solemn° hunting is in hand.
       There will the lovely Roman ladies troop:
       The forest walks are wide and spacious,
115 And many unfrequented plots° there are
       Fitted by kind° for rape and villainy.
       Single° you thither then this dainty doe,
       And strike her home by force, if not by words:
       This way, or not at all, stand you in hope.
120 Come, come, our empress, with her sacred wit
       To villainy and vengeance consecrate,
       Will we acquaint withal what we intend,
       And she shall file our engines° with advice,
       That will not suffer you to square yourselves,
125 But to your wishes' height advance you both.
       The Emperor's court is like the House of Fame,°
       The palace full of tongues, of eyes, and ears:
       The woods are ruthless,° dreadful, deaf, and dull;
       There speak, and strike, brave boys, and take your
            turns,
130   There serve your lust shadowed from heaven's eye,
       And revel in Lavinia's treasury.

103 *for that you jar* to get what you quarrel over   104 *policy* cunning   105 *affect* desire   107 *perforce* necessarily   108 *Lucrece*
Roman lady noted for her chastity; she killed herself when Sextus
Tarquinius raped her   112 *solemn* ceremonious   115 *unfrequented
plots* unvisited areas   116 *kind* nature   117 *Single* single out (a
hunting term)   123 *file our engines* sharpen our minds   126 *House
of Fame* (Ovid and Chaucer have notable poems on it; Fame =
Rumor, and the House of Fame is full of gossip)   128 *ruthless*
pitiless

Chiron. Thy counsel, lad, smells of no cowardice.

Demetrius. Sit fas aut nefas,° till I find the stream
    To cool this heat, a charm to calm these fits,
    Per Stygia, per manes vehor.°   *Exeunt.* 135

[Scene II. *A forest near Rome.*]

*Enter Titus Andronicus and his three sons [and
Marcus], making a noise with hounds and horns.*

Titus. The hunt is up, the morn is bright and gray,°
    The fields are fragrant, and the woods are green:
    Uncouple° here, and let us make a bay,°
    And wake the Emperor and his lovely bride,
    And rouse the Prince, and ring a hunter's peal,   5
    That all the court may echo with the noise.
    Sons, let it be your charge, as it is ours,
    To attend the Emperor's person carefully:
    I have been troubled in my sleep this night,
    But dawning day new comfort hath inspired.   10

Here a cry° *of hounds, and wind horns in a peal: then
    enter Saturninus, Tamora, Bassianus, Lavinia,
        Chiron, Demetrius, and their attendants.*

    Many good morrows to your Majesty!
    Madam, to you as many and as good!
    I promisèd your Grace a hunter's peal.

Saturninus. And you have rung it lustily, my lords,
    Somewhat too early for new-married ladies.   15

Bassianus. Lavinia, how say you?

---

133 *Sit fas aut nefas* be it right or wrong (Latin) 135 *Per Stygia,
per manes vehor* I am carried through Stygian (infernal) regions,
through ghosts (Latin, derived from Seneca's *Hippolytus,* line 1177)
II.ii.1 *gray* sky blue (?)   3 *Uncouple* unleash the hounds   3 *make a
bay* keep up the cry of the hounds   10 s.d. *cry* deep barking

Lavinia.   I say, no;
  I have been broad awake two hours and more.

Saturninus. Come on then, horse and chariots let us
      have,
  And to our sport. [*To Tamora*] Madam, now shall
      ye see
  Our Roman hunting.

20 *Marcus.*   I have dogs, my lord,
  Will rouse the proudest panther in the chase,
  And climb the highest promontory top.

Titus. And I have horse will follow where the game
  Makes way and runs like swallows o'er the plain.

Demetrius. Chiron, we hunt not, we, with horse nor
25   hound,
  But hope to pluck a dainty doe to ground.   *Exeunt.*

[Scene III. *The forest.*]

Enter Aaron alone, [with a bag of gold].

Aaron. He that had wit would think that I had none,
  To bury so much gold under a tree
  And never after to inherit° it.
  Let him that thinks of me so abjectly°
5 Know that this gold must coin a stratagem,
  Which, cunningly effected, will beget
  A very excellent piece of villainy.
  And so repose, sweet gold, for their unrest,
  That have their alms out of the Empress' chest.
                              [*Hides the gold.*]

Enter Tamora alone to the Moor.

10 *Tamora.* My lovely Aaron, wherefore look'st thou sad

II.iii.3 *inherit* possess   4 *abjectly* contemptuously

When every thing doth make a gleeful boast?°
The birds chaunt melody on every bush,
The snakes lies rollèd in the cheerful sun,
The green leaves quiver with the cooling wind,
And make a checkered shadow on the ground: *15*
Under their sweet shade, Aaron, let us sit,
And whilst the babbling echo mocks the hounds,
Replying shrilly to the well-tuned horns
As if a double hunt were heard at once,
Let us sit down and mark their yellowing° noise: *20*
And after conflict such as was supposed
The wandering prince and Dido° once enjoyed,
When with a happy storm they were surprised
And curtained with a counsel-keeping cave,
We may, each wreathèd in the other's arms,   *25*
(Our pastimes done) possess a golden slumber,
Whiles hounds and horns and sweet melodious birds
Be unto us as is a nurse's song
Of lullaby to bring her babe asleep.

Aaron. Madam, though Venus govern your desires,   *30*
Saturn is dominator° over mine:
What signifies my deadly-standing° eye,
My silence and my cloudy melancholy,
My fleece of woolly hair that now uncurls
Even as an adder when she doth unroll   *35*
To do some fatal execution?
No, madam, these are no venereal° signs:
Vengeance is in my heart, death in my hand,
Blood and revenge are hammering in my head.
Hark, Tamora, the empress of my soul,   *40*
Which never hopes more heaven than rests in thee,
This is the day of doom for Bassianus:
His Philomel° must lose her tongue today,

11 *boast* display   20 *yellowing* loudly calling   22 *The wandering prince and Dido* Aeneas and the Queen of Carthage (see Virgil's *Aeneid* IV)   31 *Saturn is dominator* the planet Saturn (whose influence allegedly caused sluggishness) dominates   32 *deadly-standing* fixed in a deathlike stare (?)   37 *venereal* erotic   43 *Philomel* (Philomela was ravished by Tereus, who then cut out her tongue; later she communicated her plight by weaving the story into a tapestry. See II.iv.26–27, 38–39; IV.i.47–48; V.ii.200)

Thy sons make pillage of her chastity,
45 And wash their hands in Bassianus' blood.
Seest thou this letter? Take it up, I pray thee,
And give the King this fatal-plotted scroll.
Now question me no more; we are espied.
Here comes a parcel of our hopeful booty,°
50 Which dreads not yet their lives' destruction.

Enter Bassianus and Lavinia.

Tamora. Ah, my sweet Moor, sweeter to me than life!

Aaron. No more, great Empress, Bassianus comes.
Be cross with him, and I'll go fetch thy sons
To back thy quarrels whatsoe'er they be.   [*Exit.*]

55 *Bassianus.* Who have we here? Rome's royal Empress,
Unfurnished of° her well-beseeming troop?
Or is it Dian, habited° like her,
Who hath abandonèd her holy groves
To see the general hunting in this forest?

60 *Tamora.* Saucy controller° of my private steps!
Had I the power that some say Dian had,
Thy temples should be planted presently°
With horns, as was Actaeon's,° and the hounds
Should drive upon thy new-transformèd limbs,
65 Unmannerly intruder as thou art!

Lavinia. Under your patience, gentle Empress,
'Tis thought you have a goodly gift in horning,°
And to be doubted° that your Moor and you
Are singled forth to try experiments:
70 Jove shield your husband from his hounds today!
'Tis pity they should take him for a stag.

Bassianus. Believe me, Queen, your swart Cimmerian°

49 *parcel of our hopeful booty* part of the victims we hope for
56 *Unfurnished of* unaccompanied by   57 *habited* dressed   60 *con-troller* critic   62 *presently* immediately   63 *Actaeon* legendary
hunter who spied on Diana bathing; she transformed him into a
stag and his own hounds killed him   67 *horning* (an unfaithful
wife was said to give her husband horns)   68 *doubted* suspected
72 *Cimmerian* dweller in darkness

Doth make your honor of his body's hue,
Spotted,° detested, and abominable.
Why are you sequest'rèd from all your train,　　75
Dismounted from your snow-white goodly steed,
And wand'red hither to an obscure plot,
Accompanied but with a barbarous Moor,
If foul desire had not conducted you?

Lavinia. And, being intercepted in your sport,　　80
Great reason that my noble lord be rated°
For sauciness. I pray you, let us hence,
And let her joy° her raven-colored love;
This valley fits the purpose passing well.

Bassianus. The King my brother shall have notice° of
this.　　85

Lavinia. Ay, for these slips have made him noted°
long.
Good king, to be so mightily abused!

Tamora. Why, I have patience to endure all this.

Enter Chiron and Demetrius.

Demetrius. How now, dear sovereign, and our gracious mother,
Why doth your Highness look so pale and wan?　　90

Tamora. Have I not reason, think you, to look pale?
These two have ticed° me hither to this place,
A barren detested vale, you see it is;
The trees, though summer, yet forlorn and lean,
Overcome with moss and baleful mistletoe:　　95
Here never shines the sun; here nothing breeds,
Unless the nightly owl or fatal raven:
And when they showed me this abhorrèd pit,
They told me, here, at dead time of the night
A thousand fiends, a thousand hissing snakes,　　100
Ten thousand swelling toads, as many urchins,°
Would make such fearful and confusèd cries,

74 *Spotted* infected　81 *rated* berated, rebuked　83 *joy* enjoy　85
notice (monosyllabic, pronounced "notes")　86 *noted* notorious
92 *ticed* enticed　101 *urchins* hedgehogs

As any mortal body hearing it
Should straight fall mad, or else die suddenly.
105 No sooner had they told this hellish tale,
But straight they told me they would bind me here
Unto the body of a dismal yew,
And leave me to this miserable death.
And then they called me foul adulteress,
110 Lascivious Goth,° and all the bitterest terms
That ever ear did hear to such effect.
And, had you not by wondrous fortune come,
This vengeance on me had they executed:
Revenge it, as you love your mother's life,
115 Or be ye not henceforth called my children.

Demetrius. This is a witness that I am thy son.
                 Stab[s] him.

Chiron. And this for me, struck home to show my
     strength.   *[Stabs Bassianus.]*

Lavinia. Ay come, Semiramis, nay, barbarous
     Tamora!
For no name fits thy nature but thy own!

Tamora. Give me the poniard! You shall know, my
120   boys,
Your mother's hand shall right your mother's
     wrong.

Demetrius. Stay, madam; here is more belongs to her.
First thrash the corn, then after burn the straw.
This minion stood upon° her chastity,
125 Upon her nuptial vow, her loyalty,
And with that painted° hope braves your mighti-
     ness:
And shall she carry this unto her grave?

Chiron. And if she do, I would I were an eunuch.
Drag hence her husband to some secret hole,

110 *Goth* (possibly a pun on "goat," an animal believed to be
lascivious)   124 *minion stood upon* hussy made a fuss about   126
painted specious, unreal

And make his dead trunk pillow to our lust.   130

Tamora. But when ye have the honey we desire,
Let not this wasp outlive us both to sting.

Chiron. I warrant you, madam, we will make that
    sure.
Come, mistress, now perforce we will enjoy
That nice-preservèd honesty° of yours.   135

Lavinia. O Tamora! Thou bearest a woman's face—

Tamora. I will not hear her speak; away with her.

Lavinia. Sweet lords, entreat her hear me but a word.

Demetrius. Listen, fair madam, let it be your glory
To see her tears, but be your heart to them   140
As unrelenting flint to drops of rain.

Lavinia. When did the tiger's young ones teach the
    dam?°
O, do not learn° her wrath; she taught it thee.
The milk thou suck'st from her did turn to marble;
Even at thy teat thou hadst thy tyranny.   145
Yet every mother breeds not sons alike,
[*To Chiron*] Do thou entreat her show a woman's
    pity.

Chiron. What! Wouldst thou have me prove myself
    a bastard?

Lavinia. 'Tis true; the raven doth not hatch a lark:
Yet have I heard—O could I find it now!—   150
The lion, moved with pity, did endure
To have his princely paws pared all away.
Some say that ravens foster forlorn children,
The whilst their own birds famish in their nests:
O, be to me, though thy hard heart say no,   155
Nothing so kind but something pitiful!°

---

135 *nice-preserved honesty* fastidiously guarded chastity   142 *dam*
mother   143 *learn* teach   156 *Nothing so kind but something piti-*
ful i.e., not so kind as the raven, but somewhat pitying

Tamora. I know not what it means; away with her!

Lavinia. O, let me teach thee for my father's sake,
 That gave thee life when well he might have slain
  thee.
160 Be not obdurate, open thy deaf ears.

Tamora. Hadst thou in person ne'er offended me,
 Even for his sake am I pitiless.
 Remember, boys, I poured forth tears in vain
 To save your brother from the sacrifice,
165 But fierce Andronicus would not relent.
 Therefore away with her, and use her as you will;
 The worse to her, the better loved of me.

Lavinia. O Tamora, be called a gentle queen,
 And with thine own hands kill me in this place!
170 For 'tis not life that I have begged so long;
 Poor I was slain when Bassianus died.

Tamora. What begg'st thou then? Fond° woman, let
  me go.

Lavinia. 'Tis present death I beg, and one thing more
 That womanhood denies° my tongue to tell.
175 O, keep me from their worse than killing lust,
 And tumble me into some loathsome pit,
 Where never man's eye may behold my body.
 Do this, and be a charitable murderer.

Tamora. So should I rob my sweet sons of their fee.
180 No, let them satisfice their lust on thee.

Demetrius. Away! For thou hast stayed us here too
  long.

Lavinia. No grace? No womanhood? Ah beastly crea-
  ture!
 The blot and enemy to our general name!°
 Confusion° fall—

Chiron. Nay, then I'll stop your mouth. Bring thou
185 her husband.

172 *Fond* foolish 174 *denies* forbids 183 *our general name* i.e.,
womankind 184 *Confusion* destruction

This is the hole where Aaron bid us hide him.
[Demetrius throws the corpse into a pit and then
covers it with branches. Exeunt Demetrius and
Chiron, dragging Lavinia.]

Tamora. Farewell, my sons, see that you make her
        sure.
    Ne'er let my heart know merry cheer indeed
    Till all the Andronici be made away.°
    Now will I hence to seek my lovely Moor,   190
    And let my spleenful° sons this trull° deflower.
                                              [Exit.]

Enter Aaron with two of Titus' sons [Quintus and
Martius].

[Aaron.] Come on, my lords, the better foot before!
    Straight will I bring you to the loathesome pit
    Where I espied the panther fast asleep.

Quintus. My sight is very dull, whate'er it bodes.   195

Martius. And mine, I promise you. Were it not for
        shame,
    Well could I leave our sport to sleep awhile.
                                      [He falls into the pit.]

Quintus. What, art thou fallen? What subtle hole is
        this,
    Whose mouth is covered with rude-growing briers,
    Upon whose leaves are drops of new-shed blood   200
    As fresh as morning dew distilled on flowers?
    A very fatal place it seems to me.
    Speak, brother, hast thou hurt thee with the fall?

Martius. O, brother, with the dismal'st object hurt
    That ever eye with sight made heart lament.   205

Aaron. *[Aside]* Now will I fetch the King to find them
        here,
    That he thereby may have a likely guess
    How these were they that made away his brother.
                                              Exit.

189 *made away* killed   191 *spleenful* lustful   191 *trull* strumpet

Martius. Why dost not comfort me and help me out
210   From this unhallowed and bloodstainèd hole?

Quintus. I am surprisèd° with an uncouth° fear,
    A chilling sweat o'erruns my trembling joints;
    My heart suspects more than mine eye can see.

Martius. To prove thou hast a true-divining heart,
215   Aaron and thou look down into this den
    And see a fearful sight of blood and death.

Quintus. Aaron is gone, and my compassionate heart
    Will not permit mine eyes once to behold
    The thing whereat it trembles by surmise.
220   O, tell me who it is, for ne'er till now
    Was I a child to fear I know not what.

Martius. Lord Bassianus lies berayed° in blood,
    All on a heap, like to a slaughtered lamb,
    In this detested, dark, blood-drinking pit.

225 *Quintus.* If it be dark, how dost thou know 'tis he?

Martius. Upon his bloody finger he doth wear
    A precious ring that lightens all this hole,
    Which, like a taper in some monument,
    Doth shine upon the dead man's earthy cheeks,
230   And shows the ragged entrails° of this pit:
    So pale did shine the moon on Pyramus,
    When he by night lay bathed in maiden blood.
    O brother, help me with thy fainting hand—
    If fear hath made thee faint, as me it hath—
235   Out of this fell° devouring receptacle,
    As hateful as Cocytus'° misty mouth.

Quintus. Reach me thy hand, that I may help thee out;
    Or, wanting° strength to do thee so much good,
    I may be plucked into the swallowing womb
240   Of this deep pit, poor Bassianus' grave.
    I have no strength to pluck thee to the brink.

---

211 *surprisèd* dumfounded   211 *uncouth* strange   222 *berayed* defiled   230 *ragged entrails* rugged interior   235 *fell* savage   236 *Cocytus* river in Hades   238 *wanting* lacking

Martius. Nor I no strength to climb without thy help.

Quintus. Thy hand once more; I will not loose again
　　Till thou art here aloft or I below:
　　Thou canst not come to me; I come to thee.　　245
　　　　　　　　　　　　　　　　　[Falls in.]

　　Enter the Emperor and Aaron the Moor.

Saturninus. Along with me! I'll see what hole is here,
　　And what he is that now is leaped into it.
　　Say, who art thou, that lately didst descend
　　Into this gaping hollow of the earth?

Martius. The unhappy sons of old Andronicus,　　250
　　Brought hither in a most unlucky hour,
　　To find thy brother Bassianus dead.

Saturninus. My brother dead! I know thou dost but
　　　jest:
　　He and his lady both are at the lodge,
　　Upon the north side of this pleasant chase;　　255
　　'Tis not an hour since I left them there.

Martius. We know not where you left them all alive,
　　But, out alas! Here have we found him dead.

　　Enter Tamora, Andronicus, and Lucius.

Tamora. Where is my lord the King?

Saturninus. Here, Tamora, though grieved with killing
　　　grief.　　260

Tamora. Where is thy brother, Bassianus?

Saturninus. Now to the bottom dost thou search° my
　　　wound;
　　Poor Bassianus here lies murderèd.

Tamora. Then all too late I bring this fatal writ,
　　The complot° of this timeless° tragedy;　　265
　　And wonder greatly that man's face can fold°

263 *search* probe　265 *complot* plot　265 *timeless* untimely　266
fold hide (in the creases of a hypocritical smile)

In pleasing smiles such murderous tyranny.

She giveth Saturnine a letter.

Saturninus. (Reads the letter.) "And if° we miss to
    meet him handsomely°—
Sweet huntsman, Bassianus 'tis we mean—
270 Do thou so much as dig the grave for him.
Thou know'st our meaning. Look for thy reward
Among the nettles at the elder tree
Which overshades the mouth of that same pit
Where we decreed to bury Bassianus.
275 Do this and purchase us thy lasting friends."
O, Tamora! Was ever heard the like?
This is the pit, and this the elder tree.
Look, sirs, if you can find the huntsman out
That should° have murdered Bassianus here.

280 *Aaron.* My gracious lord, here is the bag of gold.

Saturninus. [*To Titus*] Two of thy whelps, fell° curs
    of bloody kind,°
Have here bereft my brother of his life.
Sirs, drag them from the pit unto the prison,
There let them bide until we have devised
285 Some never-heard-of torturing pain for them.

Tamora. What, are they in this pit? O wondrous thing!
How easily murder is discoverèd!

Titus. High Emperor, upon my feeble knee
I beg this boon, with tears not lightly shed,
290 That this fell fault of my accursèd sons,
Accursèd, if the faults be proved in them—

Saturninus. If it be proved! You see, it is apparent.°
Who found this letter? Tamora, was it you?

Tamora. Andronicus himself did take it up.

295 *Titus.* I did, my lord, yet let me be their bail,
For by my father's reverend tomb I vow
They shall be ready at your Highness' will

268 *And if* if   268 *handsomely* handily   279 *should* was to   281
fell savage   281 *kind* nature   292 *apparent* obvious

To answer their suspicion° with their lives.

Saturninus. Thou shalt not bail them; see thou follow
me.
Some bring the murdered body, some the murderers.   *300*
Let them not speak a word; the guilt is plain,
For by my soul were there worse end than death,
That end upon them should be executed.

Tamora. Andronicus, I will entreat the King.
Fear not° thy sons; they shall do well enough.   *305*

Titus. Come, Lucius, come, stay not to talk with them.
[*Exeunt.*]

[Scene IV. *The forest.*]

*Enter the Empress' sons with Lavinia, her hands cut
off, and her tongue cut out, and ravished.*

Demetrius. So, now go tell, and if° thy tongue can
speak,
Who 'twas that cut thy tongue and ravished thee.

Chiron. Write down thy mind, bewray° thy meaning
so,
And if thy stumps will let thee play the scribe.

Demetrius. See how with signs and tokens she can
scrowl.°
                                                        5

Chiron. Go home, call for sweet° water, wash thy
hands.

Demetrius. She hath no tongue to call nor hands to
wash,
And so let's leave her to her silent walks.

298 *their suspicion* i.e., the suspicion they are under   305 *Fear not*
do not fear for   II.iv.1 *and if* if (as in line 4)   3 *bewray* reveal   5
scrowl scrawl (with a pun on "scroll"?)   6 *sweet* perfumed

Chiron. And 'twere my cause,° I should go hang
    myself.

Demetrius. If thou hadst hands to help thee knit the
10   cord.   *Exeunt* [*Chiron and Demetrius*].

Enter Marcus from hunting.

Marcus. Who is this? My niece, that flies away so fast!
    Cousin,° a word, where is your husband?
    If I do dream, would all my wealth would wake me!
    If I do wake, some planet strike me down,
15   That I may slumber an eternal sleep!
    Speak, gentle niece, what stern ungentle hands
    Hath lopped and hewed and made thy body bare
    Of her two branches, those sweet ornaments,
    Whose circling shadows kings have sought to sleep
        in,
20   And might not gain so great a happiness
    As half thy love? Why dost not speak to me?
    Alas, a crimson river of warm blood,
    Like to a bubbling fountain stirred with wind,
    Doth rise and fall between thy rosèd lips,
25   Coming and going with thy honey breath.
    But, sure, some Tereus° hath deflowered thee,
    And, lest thou shouldst detect° him, cut thy tongue.
    Ah, now thou turn'st away thy face for shame!
    And, notwithstanding all this loss of blood,
30   As from a conduit with three issuing spouts,
    Yet do thy cheeks look red as Titan's° face
    Blushing to be encount'red with a cloud.
    Shall I speak for thee? Shall I say 'tis so?
    O, that I knew thy heart, and knew the beast,
35   That I might rail at him to ease my mind!
    Sorrow concealèd, like an oven stopped,
    Doth burn the heart to cinders where it is.
    Fair Philomela, why she but lost her tongue,

9 *cause* case   12 *Cousin* (commonly used of any near relative other
than a parent, child, or sibling)   26 *Tereus* ravisher of Philomela
(see note to II.iii.43)   27 *detect* expose   31 *Titan's* the sun god's

And in a tedious sampler° sewed her mind:
But lovely niece, that mean is cut from thee;　　　*40*
A craftier Tereus, cousin, hast thou met,
And he hath cut those pretty fingers off,
That could have better sewed than Philomel.
O, had the monster seen those lily hands
Tremble like aspen leaves upon a lute,　　　*45*
And make the silken strings delight to kiss them,
He would not then have touched them for his life!
Or, had he heard the heavenly harmony
Which that sweet tongue hath made,
He would have dropped his knife, and fell asleep　　　*50*
As Cerberus° at the Thracian poet's feet.
Come, let us go and make thy father blind,
For such a sight will blind a father's eye.
One hour's storm will drown the fragrant meads;
What will whole months of tears thy father's eyes?　　　*55*
Do not draw back, for we will mourn with thee:
O, could our mourning ease thy misery!　　*Exeunt.*

---

39 *tedious sampler* laboriously executed tapestry　51 *Cerberus*
three-headed dog who guarded the entrance to Hades; he was lulled
by Orpheus, *the Thracian poet*

[ACT III

Scene I. *Rome. A street.*]

Enter the Judges and Senators with Titus' two sons bound, passing on the stage to the place of execution, and Titus going before, pleading.

Titus. Hear me, grave fathers! Noble tribunes, stay!
For pity of mine age, whose youth was spent
In dangerous wars, whilst you securely slept;
For all my blood in Rome's great quarrel shed,
5 For all the frosty nights that I have watched,
And for these bitter tears, which now you see
Filling the agèd wrinkles in my cheeks,
Be pitiful to my condemnèd sons,
Whose souls is not corrupted as 'tis thought.
10 For two and twenty sons I never wept,
Because they died in honor's lofty bed;

Andronicus lieth down° and the Judges pass by him.

For these, tribunes, in the dust I write
My heart's deep languor° and my soul's sad tears:
Let my tears staunch° the earth's dry appetite;
15 My sons' sweet blood will make it shame and blush.
O earth, I will befriend thee more with rain,
That shall distill from these two ancient ruins,
Than youthful April shall with all his show'rs:
In summer's drought I'll drop upon thee still,°

III.i.11 s.d. *lieth down* i.e., prostrates himself   13 *languor* grief
14 *staunch* satisfy, satiate   19 *still* continuously

76

In winter with warm tears I'll melt the snow,   *20*
And keep eternal springtime on thy face,
So° thou refuse to drink my dear sons' blood.

Enter Lucius, with his weapon drawn.

O reverend tribunes! O gentle agèd men!
Unbind my sons, reverse the doom° of death,
And let me say, that never wept before,   *25*
My tears are now prevailing orators.

Lucius. O noble father, you lament in vain,
The tribunes hear you not, no man is by,
And you recount your sorrows to a stone.

Titus. Ah, Lucius, for thy brothers let me plead.   *30*
Grave tribunes, once more I entreat of you.

Lucius. My gracious lord, no tribune hears you speak.

Titus. Why, 'tis no matter, man, if they did hear
They would not mark me, if they did mark
They would not pity me, yet plead I must,   *35*
And bootless° unto them.
Therefore I tell my sorrows to the stones,
Who though they cannot answer my distress,
Yet in some sort they are better than the tribunes,
For that they will not intercept° my tale: *40*
When I do weep they humbly at my feet
Receive my tears and seem to weep with me;
And were they but attirèd in grave weeds,°
Rome could afford no tribunes like to these.
A stone is soft as wax, tribunes more hard than
   stones: *45*
A stone is silent and offendeth not,
And tribunes with their tongues doom men to death.
But wherefore stand'st thou with thy weapon
   drawn?

Lucius. To rescue my two brothers from their death,
For which attempt the judges have pronounced   *50*

22 *So* provided that   24 *doom* judgment   36 *bootless* in vain   40 *intercept* interrupt   43 *grave weeds* solemn apparel

My everlasting doom of banishment.

Titus. O happy man! They have befriended thee.
Why, foolish Lucius, dost thou not perceive
That Rome is but a wilderness of tigers?
55   Tigers must prey, and Rome affords no prey
But me and mine. How happy art thou then,
From these devourers to be banishèd!
But who comes with our brother Marcus here?

Enter Marcus with Lavinia.

Marcus. Titus, prepare thy agèd eyes to weep,
60   Or if not so, thy noble heart to break.
I bring consuming sorrow to thine age.

Titus. Will it consume me? Let me see it then.

Marcus. This was thy daughter.

Titus.   Why, Marcus, so she is.

Lucius. Ay me! This object° kills me!

65   *Titus.* Faint-hearted boy, arise, and look upon her.
Speak, Lavinia, what accursèd hand
Hath made thee handless in thy father's sight?
What fool hath added water to the sea,
Or brought a faggot to bright-burning Troy?
70   My grief was at the height before thou cam'st,
And now like Nilus° it disdaineth bounds.
Give me a sword, I'll chop off my hands too,
For they have fought for Rome, and all in vain;
And they have nursed this woe, in feeding life;
75   In bootless prayer have they been held up,
And they have served me to effectless use.
Now all the service I require of them
Is that the one will help to cut the other.
'Tis well, Lavinia, that thou hast no hands,
80   For hands to do Rome service is but vain.

Lucius. Speak, gentle sister, who hath mart'red° thee?

Marcus. O, that delightful engine° of her thoughts,

64 *object* sight   71 *Nilus* the Nile   81 *mart'red* mutilated   82
engine instrument

That blabbed° them with such pleasing eloquence,
Is torn from forth that pretty hollow cage,
Where like a sweet melodious bird it sung   85
Sweet varied notes, enchanting every ear!

Lucius. O, say thou for her, who hath done this deed?

Marcus. O, thus I found her, straying in the park,
Seeking to hide herself, as doth the deer
That hath received some unrecuring° wound.   90

Titus. It was my dear, and he that wounded her
Hath hurt me more than had he killed me dead:
For now I stand as one upon a rock,
Environed with a wilderness of sea,
Who marks the waxing tide grow wave by wave,   95
Expecting ever when some envious° surge
Will in his brinish bowels swallow him.
This way to death my wretched sons are gone,
Here stands my other son, a banished man,
And here my brother weeping at my woes: 100
But that which gives my soul the greatest spurn°
Is dear Lavinia, dearer than my soul.
Had I but seen thy picture in this plight,
It would have madded me: what shall I do
Now I behold thy lively° body so?   105
Thou hast no hands to wipe away thy tears,
Nor tongue to tell me who hath mart'red thee.
Thy husband he is dead, and for his death
Thy brothers are condemned, and dead by this.°
Look, Marcus! Ah, son Lucius, look on her!   110
When I did name her brothers, then fresh tears
Stood on her cheeks, as doth the honey-dew
Upon a gath'red lily almost withered.

Marcus. Perchance she weeps because they killed her
husband,
Perchance because she knows them innocent.   115

---

83 *blabbed* freely spoke   90 *unrecuring* incurable   96 *envious* malicious   101 *spurn* thrust   105 *lively* living   109 *by this* by this time

Titus. If they did kill thy husband, then be joyful,
 Because the law hath ta'en revenge on them.
 No, no, they would not do so foul a deed;
 Witness the sorrow that their sister makes.
120 Gentle Lavinia, let me kiss thy lips,
 Or make some sign how I may do thee ease.°
 Shall thy good uncle, and thy brother Lucius,
 And thou, and I, sit round about some fountain,
 Looking all downwards, to behold our cheeks
125 How they are stained, like meadows yet not dry
 With miry slime left on them by a flood?
 And in the fountain shall we gaze so long
 Till the fresh taste be taken from that clearness,°
 And made a brine-pit with our bitter tears?
130 Or shall we cut away our hands, like thine?
 Or shall we bite our tongues, and in dumb shows°
 Pass the remainder of our hateful days?
 What shall we do? Let us, that have our tongues,
 Plot some device of further misery,
135 To make us wondered at in time to come.

Lucius. Sweet father, cease your tears, for at your
  grief
 See how my wretched sister sobs and weeps.

Marcus. Patience, dear niece. Good Titus, dry thine
  eyes.

Titus. Ah, Marcus, Marcus! Brother, well I wot
140 Thy napkin° cannot drink a tear of mine,
 For thou, poor man, hast drowned it with thine own.

Lucius. Ah, my Lavinia, I will wipe thy cheeks.

Titus. Mark, Marcus, mark! I understand her signs:
 Had she a tongue to speak, now would she say
145 That to her brother which I said to thee:
 His napkin, with his true tears all bewet,
 Can do no service on her sorrowful cheeks.
 O, what a sympathy° of woe is this!

121 *do thee ease* bring you relief 128 *clearness* i.e., clear pool 131
dumb shows silent signs 140 *napkin* handkerchief 148 *sympathy*
agreement

As far from help as Limbo is from bliss!

Enter Aaron the Moor alone.

Aaron. Titus Andronicus, my lord the Emperor   *150*
  Sends thee this word, that, if thou love thy sons,
  Let Marcus, Lucius, or thyself, old Titus,
  Or any one of you, chop off your hand
  And send it to the King: he for the same
  Will send thee hither both thy sons alive,   *155*
  And that shall be the ransom for their fault.

Titus. O, gracious Emperor! O, gentle Aaron!
  Did ever raven sing so like a lark,
  That gives sweet tidings of the sun's uprise?
  With all my heart, I'll send the Emperor my hand.   *160*
  Good Aaron, wilt thou help to chop it off?

Lucius. Stay, father! For that noble hand of thine
  That hath thrown down so many enemies
  Shall not be sent; my hand will serve the turn.
  My youth can better spare my blood than you,   *165*
  And therefore mine shall save my brothers' lives.

Marcus. Which of your hands hath not defended Rome
  And reared aloft the bloody battle-ax,
  Writing destruction on the enemy's castle?
  O, none of both but are of high desert: *170*
  My hand hath been but idle; let it serve
  To ransom my two nephews from their death,
  Then have I kept it to a worthy end.

Aaron. Nay, come, agree whose hand shall go along,
  For fear they die before their pardon come.   *175*

Marcus. My hand shall go.

Lucius.   By heaven, it shall not go.

Titus. Sirs, strive no more; such with'red herbs as these
  Are meet° for plucking up, and therefore mine.

Lucius. Sweet father, if I shall be thought thy son,
  Let me redeem my brothers both from death.   *180*

178 *meet* fit

Marcus. And, for our father's sake and mother's care,
Now let me show a brother's love to thee.

Titus. Agree between you; I will spare my hand.

Lucius. Then I'll go fetch an ax.

185 *Marcus.* But I will use the ax.
                              Exeunt [Lucius and Marcus].

Titus. Come hither, Aaron. I'll deceive them both;
Lend me thy hand, and I will give thee mine.

Aaron. [*Aside*] If that be called deceit, I will be honest,
And never whilst I live deceive men so:
190 But I'll deceive you in another sort,
And that you'll say, ere half an hour pass.
                              He cuts off Titus' hand.

          Enter Lucius and Marcus again.

Titus. Now stay your strife, what shall be is dispatched.
Good Aaron, give his Majesty my hand;
Tell him it was a hand that warded° him
195 From thousand dangers; bid him bury it;
More hath it merited, that let it have.
As for my sons, say I account of them
As jewels purchased at an easy price,
And yet dear too because I bought mine own.

200 *Aaron.* I go, Andronicus, and for thy hand
Look by and by to have thy sons with thee.
[*Aside*] Their heads, I mean. O, how this villainy
Doth fat° me with the very thoughts of it!
Let fools do good, and fair men call for grace,
205 Aaron will have his soul black like his face.   *Exit.*

Titus. O, here I lift this one hand up to heaven,
And bow this feeble ruin to the earth.
If any power pities wretched tears,
To that I call! [*To Lavinia*] What, wouldst thou
kneel with me?

194 *warded* guarded   203 *fat* delight (literally: "nourish")

Do then, dear heart, for heaven shall hear our
   prayers,   210
Or with our sighs we'll breathe the welkin dim,°
And stain the sun with fog, as sometime clouds
When they do hug him in their melting bosoms.

Marcus. O brother, speak with possibility,
   And do not break into these deep extremes.   215

Titus. Is not my sorrow deep, having no bottom?
   Then be my passions° bottomless with them.

Marcus. But yet let reason govern thy lament.

Titus. If there were reason for these miseries,
   Then into limits could I bind my woes: 220
   When heaven doth weep, doth not the earth
     o'erflow?
   If the winds rage, doth not the sea wax mad,
   Threat'ning the welkin with his big-swoll'n face?
   And wilt thou have a reason for this coil?°
   I am the sea; hark, how her sighs doth flow!   225
   She is the weeping welkin, I the earth:
   Then must my sea be movèd with her sighs,
   Then must my earth with her continual tears
   Become a deluge, overflowed and drowned,
   For why° my bowels° cannot hide her woes,   230
   But like a drunkard must I vomit them.
   Then give me leave, for losers will have leave
   To ease their stomachs° with their bitter tongues.

Enter a Messenger, with two heads and a hand.

Messenger. Worthy Andronicus, ill art thou repaid
   For that good hand thou sent'st the Emperor.   235
   Here are the heads of thy two noble sons,
   And here's thy hand in scorn to thee sent back;
   Thy grief their sports, thy resolution mocked:

211 *breathe the welkin dim* becloud the heavens with our breath
217 *passions* outbursts   224 *coil* fuss   230 *For why* because   230
bowels (thought to be the seat of compassion; akin to the modern
use of "heart")   233 *stomachs* feeling

That° woe is me to think upon thy woes,
240   More than remembrance of my father's death.
[*Exit.*]

Marcus. Now let hot Etna cool in Sicily,
And be my heart an ever-burning hell!
These miseries are more than may be borne!
To weep with them that weep doth ease some deal,°
245   But sorrow flouted at is double death.

Lucius. Ah, that this sight should make so deep a
wound,
And yet detested life not shrink° thereat!
That ever death should let life bear his name,°
Where life hath no more interest but to breathe!
[*Lavinia kisses Titus.*]

250   *Marcus.* Alas, poor heart, that kiss is comfortless
As frozen water to a starvèd° snake.

Titus. When will this fearful slumber° have an end?

Marcus. Now, farewell, flatt'ry, die Andronicus,
Thou dost not slumber: see thy two sons' heads,
255   Thy warlike hand, thy mangled daughter here,
Thy other banished son with this dear° sight
Struck pale and bloodless, and thy brother, I,
Even like a stony image cold and numb.
Ah! Now no more will I control thy griefs:
260   Rend off thy silver hair, thy other hand
Gnawing with thy teeth, and be this dismal sight
The closing up of our most wretched eyes:
Now is a time to storm; why art thou still?

Titus. Ha, ha, ha!

Marcus. Why dost thou laugh? It fits not with this
265   hour.

Titus. Why, I have not another tear to shed.
Besides, this sorrow is an enemy,

239 *That* so that   244 *some deal* somewhat   247 *shrink* slip away
248 *bear his name* i.e., be called "life"   251 *starvèd* numbed
252 *fearful slumber* i.e., nightmare existence   256 *dear* heartfelt

And would usurp upon my wat'ry eyes
And make them blind with tributary° tears;
Then which way shall I find Revenge's Cave?   270
For these two heads do seem to speak to me,
And threat me I shall never come to bliss
Till all these mischiefs be returned again,
Even in their throats that hath committed them.
Come, let me see what task I have to do.   275
You heavy° people, circle me about,
That I may turn me to each one of you,
And swear unto my soul to right your wrongs.
The vow is made. Come, brother, take a head;
And in this hand the other will I bear.   280
And Lavinia, thou shalt be employed in these arms,
Bear thou my hand, sweet wench, between thy
          teeth:°
As for thee, boy, go, get thee from my sight.
Thou art an exile, and thou must not stay.
Hie to the Goths, and raise an army there,   285
And, if ye love me, as I think you do,
Let's kiss and part, for we have much to do.
                              Exeunt [all but Lucius].

Lucius. Farewell, Andronicus, my noble father,
The woefull'st man that ever lived in Rome!
Farewell, proud Rome, till Lucius come again;   290
He loves his pledges dearer than his life.
Farewell, Lavinia, my noble sister;
O, would thou wert as thou tofore° hast been!
But now nor Lucius nor° Lavinia lives
But in oblivion and hateful griefs.   295
If Lucius live, he will requite your wrongs,
And make proud Saturnine and his empress
Beg at the gates, like Tarquin° and his queen.

269 *tributary* paid as tribute   276 *heavy* sad   282 *teeth* (possibly Shakespeare intended to delete "teeth" from the manuscript, and substituted the less grotesque "arms" above it; if so, the compositor mistakenly took "arms" to be part of the previous line, and to make sense of it he perhaps altered something like "employed in this" to "employed in these arms")   293 *tofore* formerly   294 *nor . . . nor* neither . . . nor   298 *Tarquin* Roman king whose rule was overthrown when his son (of the same name) raped Lucrece

Now will I to the Goths and raise a pow'r,
300 To be revenged on Rome and Saturnine.

                                        Exit Lucius.

[Scene II. *Rome. Within Titus' house.*]

*A banket.° Enter Andronicus, Marcus, Lavinia,
        and the boy [Lucius].*

Titus. So, so, now sit, and look you eat no more
        Than will preserve just so much strength in us
        As will revenge these bitter woes of ours.
        Marcus, unknit that sorrow-wreathen knot:°
5   Thy niece and I, poor creatures, want our hands,
        And cannot passionate° our tenfold grief
        With folded arms. This poor right hand of mine
        Is left to tyrannize upon my breast;
        Who, when my heart all mad with misery
10   Beats in this hollow prison of my flesh,
        Then thus I thump it down.
        [*To Lavinia*] Thou map° of woe, that thus dost talk
              in signs,
        When thy poor heart beats with outrageous beating,
        Thou canst not strike it thus to make it still.
15   Wound it with sighing,° girl, kill it with groans;
        Or get some little knife between thy teeth,
        And just against thy heart make thou a hole,
        That all the tears that thy poor eyes let fall
        May run into that sink,° and soaking in
20   Drown the lamenting fool° in sea-salt tears.

Marcus. Fie, brother, fie! Teach her not thus to lay
        Such violent hands upon her tender life.

III.ii.s.d. *banket* light meal   4 *knot* i.e., Marcus' folded arms, a sign
of heavy thoughts   6 *passionate* passionately express   12 *map* picture   15 *wound it with sighing* (sighing was believed to shorten life)
19 *sink* sewer   20 *fool* (here, as often, implying affection and pity)

Titus. How now! Has sorrow made thee dote already?
   Why, Marcus, no man should be mad but I.
   What violent hands can she lay on her life!   *25*
   Ah, wherefore dost thou urge the name of hands,
   To bid Aeneas° tell the tale twice o'er,
   How Troy was burnt and he made miserable?
   O, handle not the theme, to talk of hands,
   Lest we remember still that we have none.   *30*
   Fie, fie, how franticly I square° my talk,
   As if we should forget we had no hands,
   If Marcus did not name the word of hands!
   Come, let's fall to; and, gentle girl, eat this.
   Here is no drink? Hark, Marcus, what she says—   *35*
   I can interpret all her martyred signs—
   She says she drinks no other drink but tears,
   Brewed with her sorrow, meshed° upon her cheeks.
   Speechless complainer, I will learn thy thought;
   In thy dumb action will I be as perfect°   *40*
   As begging hermits in their holy prayers:
   Thou shalt not sigh, nor hold thy stumps to heaven,
   Nor wink,° nor nod, nor kneel, nor make a sign,
   But I of these will wrest an alphabet,
   And by still° practice learn to know thy meaning.   *45*

Boy. Good grandsire, leave these bitter deep laments.
   Make my aunt merry with some pleasing tale.

Marcus. Alas, the tender boy, in passion moved,
   Doth weep to see his grandsire's heaviness.

Titus. Peace, tender sapling, thou art made of tears,   *50*
   And tears will quickly melt thy life away.
         Marcus strikes the dish with a knife.
   What dost thou strike at, Marcus, with thy knife?

Marcus. At that that I have killed, my lord—a fly.

Titus. Out on thee, murderer! Thou kill'st my heart;
   Mine eyes are cloyed with view of tyranny: *55*
   A deed of death done on the innocent

27 *Aeneas* (see Virgil's *Aeneid* II.2)   31 *square* shape   38 *meshed*
mashed, brewed   40 *perfect* fully knowing   43 *wink* shut the eyes
45 *still* constant

Becomes not Titus' brother. Get thee gone;
I see thou art not for my company.

Marcus. Alas, my lord, I have but killed a fly.

60 *Titus.* "But!" How, if that fly had a father and mother?
How would he hang his slender gilded wings,
And buzz lamenting doings in the air!
Poor harmless fly,
That, with his pretty buzzing melody,
Came here to make us merry! And thou hast killed
65 him.

Marcus. Pardon me, sir; it was a black ill-favored°
fly,
Like to the Empress' Moor. Therefore I killed him.

Titus. O, O, O,
Then pardon me for reprehending thee,
70 For thou hast done a charitable deed.
Give me thy knife, I will insult on° him,
Flattering myself, as if it were the Moor,
Come hither purposely to poison me.
                              [*He strikes at it.*]
There's for thyself, and that's for Tamora.
75 Ah, sirrah!°
Yet I think we are not brought so low
But that between us we can kill a fly
That comes in likeness of a coal-black Moor.

Marcus. Alas, poor man! Grief has so wrought on
him,
80 He takes false shadows for true substances.

Titus. Come, take away.° Lavinia, go with me:
I'll to thy closet,° and go read with thee
Sad stories chancèd° in the times of old.
Come, boy, and go with me; thy sight is young,
85 And thou shalt read when mine begin to dazzle.
                                        Exeunt.

66 *ill-favored* ugly   71 *insult on* exult over   75 *sirrah* (common
term of address to an inferior)   81 *take away* clear the table   82
closet private room   83 *chancèd* that happened

[ACT IV

Scene I. *Rome. Before Titus' house.*]

*Enter Lucius' son and Lavinia running after him;
and the boy flies from her with his books under
his arm. Enter Titus and Marcus.*

Boy. Help, grandsire, help! My aunt Lavinia
Follows me everywhere, I know not why.
Good uncle Marcus, see how swift she comes.
Alas, sweet aunt, I know not what you mean.

Marcus. Stand by me, Lucius, do not fear thine aunt.   5

Titus. She loves thee, boy, too well to do thee harm.

Boy. Ay, when my father was in Rome she did.

Marcus. What means my niece Lavinia by these signs?

Titus. Fear her not, Lucius. Somewhat doth she mean.
See, Lucius, see, how much she makes of thee: 10
Somewhither would she have thee go with her.
Ah, boy, Cornelia° never with more care
Read to her sons than she hath read to thee
Sweet poetry and Tully's *Orator*.°
Canst thou not guess wherefore she plies thee thus?   15

Boy. My lord, I know not, I, nor can I guess,
Unless some fit or frenzy do possess her:
For I have heard my grandsire say full oft,

IV.i.12 *Cornelia* mother of the Gracchi, two famous tribunes   14
Tully's Orator Cicero's *De oratore* (or his *Orator ad M. Brutum*)

Extremity of griefs would make men mad;
20 And I have read that Hecuba of Troy
Ran mad for sorrow. That made me to fear,
Although, my lord, I know my noble aunt
Loves me as dear as e'er my mother did,
And would not, but in fury,° fright my youth,
25 Which made me down to throw my books and fly,
Causeless perhaps. But pardon me, sweet aunt:
And, madam, if my uncle Marcus go,
I will most willingly attend° your ladyship.

Marcus. Lucius, I will.

30 *Titus.* How now, Lavinia? Marcus, what means this?
Some book there is that she desires to see.
Which is it, girl, of these? Open them, boy.
But thou art deeper read, and better skilled.
Come, and take choice of all my library,
35 And so beguile thy sorrow, till the heavens
Reveal the damned contriver of this deed.
Why lifts she up her arms in sequence thus?

Marcus. I think she means that there were more than
one
Confederate in the fact.° Ay, more there was,
40 Or else to heaven she heaves them for revenge.

Titus. Lucius, what book is that she tosseth° so?

Boy. Grandsire, 'tis Ovid's *Metamorphosis;*°
My mother gave it me.

Marcus. For love of her that's gone,
Perhaps she culled it from among the rest.

45 *Titus.* Soft! So busily she turns the leaves!
Help her! What would she find? Lavinia, shall I
read?
This is the tragic tale of Philomel,
And treats of Tereus' treason and his rape;

24 *but in fury* except in madness   28 *attend* wait on   39 *fact* crime
41 *tosseth* turns the pages of   42 *Metamorphosis* (so spelled in the
title of an Elizabethan translation by Golding, with which Shakespeare was familiar; properly *Metamorphoses*)

And rape, I fear, was root of thy annoy.

Marcus. See, brother, see, note how she quotes° the
    leaves.   *50*

Titus. Lavinia, wert thou thus surprised, sweet girl,
    Ravished and wronged, as Philomela was,
    Forced in the ruthless, vast,° and gloomy woods?
    See, see!
    Ay, such a place there is, where we did hunt—   *55*
    O, had we never, never hunted there—
    Patterned by° that the poet here describes,
    By nature made for murders and for rapes.

Marcus. O, why should nature build so foul a den,
    Unless the gods delight in tragedies?   *60*

Titus. Give signs, sweet girl, for here are none but
    friends,
    What Roman lord it was durst do the deed:
    Or slunk not Saturnine, as Tarquin erst,°
    That left the camp to sin in Lucrece' bed?

Marcus. Sit down, sweet niece: brother, sit down by
    me.   *65*
    Apollo, Pallas, Jove, or Mercury,
    Inspire me, that I may this treason find!
    My lord, look here: look here, Lavinia.
              He writes his name with his staff,
               and guides it with feet and mouth.
    This sandy plot is plain;° guide if thou canst,
    This after me.° I have writ my name   *70*
    Without the help of any hand at all.
    Cursed be that heart that forced us to this shift!°
    Write thou, good niece, and here display at last
    What God will have discovered° for revenge.
    Heaven guide thy pen to print thy sorrows plain,   *75*
    That we may know the traitors and the truth!
             She takes the staff in her mouth and guides
                 it with her stumps and writes.

50 *quotes* examines   53 *vast* desolate   57 *Patterned by* after the
pattern   63 *erst* once   69 *plain* flat   70 *after me* as I do   72 *shift*
device   74 *discovered* revealed

O, do ye read, my lord, what she hath writ?

[*Titus.*] "*Stuprum.*° Chiron. Demetrius."

Marcus. What, what! The lustful sons of Tamora
80 Performers of this heinous, bloody deed?

Titus. Magni Dominator poli,
Tam lentus audis scelera? tam lentus vides?°

Marcus. O, calm thee, gentle lord! Although I know
There is enough written upon this earth
85 To stir a mutiny in the mildest thoughts,
And arm the minds of infants to exclaims.°
My lord, kneel down with me; Lavinia, kneel;
And kneel, sweet boy, the Roman Hector's° hope;
And swear with me, as, with the woeful fere°
90 And father of that chaste dishonored dame,
Lord Junius Brutus° sware for Lucrece' rape,
That we will prosecute by good advice°
Mortal revenge upon these traitorous Goths,
And see their blood, or die with this reproach.

95 *Titus.* 'Tis sure enough, and you knew how,
But if you hunt these bear-whelps, then beware:
The dam will wake; and if she wind ye° once,
She's with the lion deeply still in league,
And lulls him whilst she playeth on her back,
100 And when he sleeps will she do what she list.°
You are a young huntsman, Marcus, let alone;
And, come, I will go get a leaf of brass,
And with a gad° of steel will write these words,
And lay it by. The angry northern wind
105 Will blow these sands like Sibyl's leaves° abroad,
And where's our lesson then? Boy, what say you?

Boy. I say, my lord, that if I were a man,

78 *Stuprum* rape (Latin)   81–82 *Magni Dominator . . . lentus*
vides? ruler of the great heavens, are you so slow to hear and to see
crimes? (Latin; derived from Seneca's *Hippolytus*, lines 668–69)
86 *exclaims* exclamations   88 *the Roman Hector's* i.e., Andronicus
(Titus is compared to Hector, Troy's champion)   89 *fere* spouse
91 *Junius Brutus* chief of those who drove the Tarquins from Rome
92 *by good advice* after careful deliberation   97 *and if she wind ye*
if she get wind of (smell) you   100 *list* please   103 *gad* spike,
stylus   105 *Sibyl's leaves* leaves on which the Sibyl wrote prophecies

Their mother's bedchamber should not be safe
For these base bondmen to the yoke of Rome.

Marcus. Ay, that's my boy! Thy father hath full oft   *110*
For his ungrateful country done the like.

Boy. And, uncle, so will I, and if I live.

Titus. Come, go with me into mine armory:
Lucius, I'll fit thee, and withal my boy
Shall carry from me to the Empress' sons   *115*
Presents that I intend to send them both.
Come, come; thou'lt do my message, wilt thou not?

Boy. Ay, with my dagger in their bosoms, grandsire.

Titus. No, boy, not so; I'll teach thee another course.
Lavinia, come. Marcus, look to my house.   *120*
Lucius and I'll go brave it° at the court;
Ay, marry,° will we, sir; and we'll be waited on.°
                                        Exeunt.

Marcus. O heavens, can you hear a good man groan,
And not relent, or not compassion him?
Marcus, attend him in his ecstasy,°   *125*
That hath more scars of sorrow in his heart
Than foemen's marks upon his batt'red shield,
But yet so just that he will not revenge.
Revenge the heavens° for old Andronicus!   *Exit.*

---

121 *brave it* behave defiantly   122 *marry* (an interjection, from "By
the Virgin Mary")   122 *be waited on* i.e., not be ignored   125
ecstasy fit of madness   129 *Revenge the heavens* may the heavens
take revenge

[Scene II. *Rome. Within the palace.*]

*Enter Aaron, Chiron, and Demetrius, at one
door, and at the other door young Lucius and
another, with a bundle of weapons and verses
writ upon them.*

Chiron. Demetrius, here's the son of Lucius,
He hath some message to deliver us.

Aaron. Ay, some mad message from his mad grandfather.

Boy. My lords, with all the humbleness I may,
5   I greet your honors from Andronicus.
       [*Aside*] And pray the Roman gods confound° you
       both.

Demetrius. Gramercy,° lovely Lucius, what's the
       news?

Boy. [*Aside*] That you are both deciphered, that's the
       news,
       For villains marked with rape. [*Aloud*] May it
       please you,
10   My grandsire, well-advised,° hath sent by me
       The goodliest weapons of his armory
       To gratify your honorable youth,
       The hope of Rome; for so he bid me say;
       And so I do, and with his gifts present
15   Your lordships; whenever you have need,
       You may be armèd and appointed° well.
       And so I leave you both, [*aside*] like bloody villains.
                                                    Exit.

Demetrius. What's here? A scroll, and written round
       about?

IV.ii.6 *confound* destroy   7 *Gramercy* thanks   10 *well-advised* in
sound mind   16 *appointed* equipped

Let's see:

> Integer vitae, scelerisque purus,   20
> Non eget Mauri jaculis, nec arcu.°

Chiron. O, 'tis a verse in Horace; I know it well:
  I read it in the grammar long ago.

Aaron. Ay, just; a verse in Horace; right, you have it.
  [Aside] Now, what a thing it is to be an ass!   25
  Here's no sound jest! The old man hath found their
    guilt,
  And sends them weapons wrapped about with lines
  That wound, beyond their feeling, to the quick.
  But were our witty° empress well afoot,
  She would applaud Andronicus' conceit.°   30
  But let her rest in her unrest awhile.
  [Aloud] And now, young lords, was't not a happy
    star
  Led us to Rome, strangers, and more than so,
  Captives, to be advancèd to this height?
  It did me good, before the palace gate   35
  To brave the tribune in his brother's hearing.

Demetrius. But me more good, to see so great a lord
  Basely insinuate° and send us gifts.

Aaron. Had he not reason, Lord Demetrius?
  Did you not use his daughter very friendly?   40

Demetrius. I would we had a thousand Roman dames
  At such a bay,° by turn to serve our lust.

Chiron. A charitable wish and full of love.

Aaron. Here lacks but your mother for to say amen.

Chiron. And that would she for twenty thousand
  more.   45

Demetrius. Come, let us go, and pray to all the gods
  For our belovèd mother in her pains.

20–21 Integer vitae . . . nec arcu the man of upright life and free
from crime has no need of a Moor's javelins or bow (Latin; from
Horace, Odes, I.xxii.1–2) 29 witty wise 30 conceit idea, design
38 insinuate curry favor 42 At such a bay thus cornered

Aaron. [*Aside*] Pray to the devils, the gods have given
us over.

Trumpets sound.

Demetrius. Why do the Emperor's trumpets flourish
thus?

50 *Chiron.* Belike,° for joy the Emperor hath a son.

Demetrius. Soft! Who comes here?

Enter Nurse with a blackamoor child.

Nurse.   God morrow, lords.
O, tell me, did you see Aaron the Moor?

Aaron. Well, more or less, or ne'er a whit at all,
Here Aaron is; and what with Aaron now?

55 *Nurse.* O gentle Aaron, we are all undone!
Now help, or woe betide thee evermore!

Aaron. Why, what a caterwauling dost thou keep!
What dost thou wrap and fumble° in thy arms?

Nurse. O, that which I would hide from heaven's eye,
60 Our empress' shame and stately Rome's disgrace!
She is delivered, lords, she is delivered.

Aaron. To whom?

Nurse.   I mean, she is brought abed.

Aaron. Well, God give her good rest! What hath he
sent her?

Nurse. A devil.

Aaron.   Why, then she is the devil's dam;°
65 A joyful issue.

Nurse. A joyless, dismal, black, and sorrowful issue!
Here is the babe, as loathsome as a toad
Amongst the fair-faced breeders of our clime.
The Empress sends it thee, thy stamp, thy seal,

50 *Belike* probably 58 *fumble* clumsily bundle up 64 *dam* mother

And bids thee christen it with thy dagger's point.   70

Aaron. Zounds,° ye whore! Is black so base a hue?
   Sweet blowse,° you are a beauteous blossom, sure.

Demetrius. Villain, what hast thou done?

Aaron. That which thou canst not undo.

Chiron. Thou hast undone our mother.   75

Aaron. Villain, I have done° thy mother.

Demetrius. And therein, hellish dog, thou hast undone
      her.
   Woe to her chance,° and damned her loathèd
      choice!
   Accursed the offspring of so foul a fiend!

Chiron. It shall not live.   80

Aaron. It shall not die.

Nurse. Aaron, it must; the mother wills it so.

Aaron. What, must it, nurse? Then let no man but I
   Do execution on my flesh and blood.

Demetrius. I'll broach° the tadpole on my rapier's
      point.   85
   Nurse, give it me; my sword shall soon dispatch it.

Aaron. Sooner this sword shall plow thy bowels up.
   Stay, murderous villains! Will you kill your brother?
   Now, by the burning tapers of the sky,
   That shone so brightly when this boy was got,°   90
   He dies upon my scimitar's sharp point
   That touches this my first-born son and heir!
   I tell you, younglings, not Enceladus,°
   With all his threat'ning band of Typhon's brood,
   Nor great Alcides,° nor the god of war,   95
   Shall seize this prey out of his father's hands.

71 *Zounds* (an interjection, from "By God's wounds")   72 *blowse*
ruddy wench (here, ironic)   76 *done* had sexual intercourse with
78 *chance* luck   85 *broach* impale   90 *got* begat   93 *Enceladus*
one of the Titans (sons of Typhon) who fought the Olympians   95
Alcides Hercules

What, what, ye sanguine,° shallow-hearted boys!
Ye white-limed walls!° Ye alehouse painted signs!
Coal-black is better than another hue,
In that it scorns to bear another hue;
For all the water in the ocean
Can never turn the swan's black legs to white,
Although she lave° them hourly in the flood.
Tell the Empress from me, I am of age
To keep mine own, excuse it how she can.

Demetrius. Wilt thou betray thy noble mistress thus?

Aaron. My mistress is my mistress, this my self,
The vigor and the picture of my youth:
This before all the world do I prefer;
This mauger° all the world will I keep safe,
Or some of you shall smoke° for it in Rome.

Demetrius. By this our mother is forever shamed.

Chiron. Rome will despise her for this foul escape.°

Nurse. The Emperor in his rage will doom her death.

Chiron. I blush to think upon this ignomy.°

Aaron. Why, there's the privilege your beauty bears:
Fie, treacherous hue, that will betray with blushing
The close enacts° and counsels of thy heart!
Here's a young lad framed of another leer:°
Look, how the black slave smiles upon the father,
As who should say, "Old lad, I am thine own."
He is your brother, lords, sensibly fed
Of that self blood° that first gave life to you,
And from your womb where you imprisoned were
He is enfranchisèd and come to light:
Nay, he is your brother by the surer side,°
Although my seal be stampèd in his face.

97 *sanguine* pink-cheeked   98 *white-limed walls* (perhaps a reference to the "whited sepulchers" of Matthew 23:27)   103 *lave* wash
110 *mauger* in spite of   111 *smoke* suffer   113 *escape* escapade
115 *ignomy* ignominy   118 *close enacts* secret resolutions   119
leer complexion   122–23 *sensibly fed/Of that self blood* i.e., his
body draws on the same blood   126 *the surer side* i.e., the mother's
side

Nurse. Aaron, what shall I say unto the Empress?

Demetrius. Advise thee, Aaron, what is to be done,
    And we will all subscribe° to thy advice: *130*
    Save thou the child, so° we may all be safe.

Aaron. Then sit we down and let us all consult.
    My son and I will have the wind of you:°
    Keep there; now talk at pleasure of your safety.

Demetrius. How many women saw this child of his?   *135*

Aaron. Why, so, brave lords! When we join in league,
    I am a lamb: but if you brave the Moor,
    The chafèd° boar, the mountain lioness,
    The ocean swells not so as Aaron storms.
    But say again, how many saw the child?   *140*

Nurse. Cornelia the midwife, and myself,
    And no one else but the delivered Empress.

Aaron. The Empress, the midwife, and yourself:
    Two may keep counsel when the third's away.
    Go to the Empress, tell her this I said.   *145*

                                        He kills her.

    Wheak, wheak!
    So cries a pig preparèd to the spit.

Demetrius. What mean'st thou, Aaron? Wherefore
    didst thou this?

Aaron. O, lord, sir, 'tis a deed of policy!°
    Shall she live to betray this guilt of ours?   *150*
    A long-tongued babbling gossip? No, lords, no.
    And now be it known to you my full intent.
    Not far one Muliteus my countryman
    His° wife but yesternight was brought to bed;
    His child is like to her, fair as you are.   *155*
    Go pack° with him, and give the mother gold,
    And tell them both the circumstance of all,°

130 *subscribe* agree   131 *so* provided that   133 *have the wind of you* i.e., keep you safely in our view (as game is watched, down wind)   138 *chafèd* enraged   149 *policy* cunning   153–54 *countryman/His* countryman's   156 *pack* conspire   157 *circumstance of all* all the details

And how by this their child shall be advanced,
And be receivèd for the Emperor's heir,
160 And substituted in the place of mine,
To calm this tempest whirling in the court;
And let the Emperor dandle him for his own.
Hark ye, lords; you see I have given her physic,°
And you must needs bestow her funeral;
165 The fields are near, and you are gallant grooms.
This done, see that you take no longer days,°
But send the midwife presently to me.
The midwife and the nurse well made away,
Then let the ladies tattle what they please.

170 *Chiron.* Aaron, I see, thou wilt not trust the air
With secrets.

Demetrius.   For this care of Tamora,
Herself and hers are highly bound to thee. *Exeunt.*

Aaron. Now to the Goths, as swift as swallow flies,
There to dispose this treasure in mine arms,
175 And secretly to greet the Empress' friends.
Come on, you thick-lipped slave, I'll bear you
hence;
For it is you that puts us to our shifts.°
I'll make you feed on berries and on roots,
And feed on curds and whey, and suck the goat,
180 And cabin° in a cave, and bring you up
To be a warrior and command a camp.   *Exit.*

163 *physic* medicine 166 *days* time 177 *puts us to our shifts*
causes us to use stratagems 180 *cabin* dwell

[Scene III. *Rome. A street.*]

*Enter Titus, old Marcus, [his son Publius,] young
Lucius, and other gentlemen, with bows; and
Titus bears the arrows with letters on the ends
of them.*

Titus. Come, Marcus, come; kinsmen, this is the way.
　　Sir boy, let me see your archery;
　　Look ye draw home° enough, and 'tis there straight.
　　Terras Astraea reliquit.°
　　Be you rememb'red,° Marcus: she's gone, she's
　　　fled.　　　　　　　　　　　　　　　　　　　　　*5*
　　Sirs, take you to your tools. You, cousins, shall
　　Go sound the ocean, and cast your nets;
　　Happily° you may catch her in the sea;
　　Yet there's as little justice as at land:
　　No, Publius and Sempronius, you must do it;　　*10*
　　'Tis you must dig with mattock and with spade,
　　And pierce the inmost center of the earth:
　　Then, when you come to Pluto's region,°
　　I pray you deliver him this petition:　　　　　　　*15*
　　Tell him, it is for justice and for aid,
　　And that it comes from old Andronicus,
　　Shaken with sorrows in ungrateful Rome.
　　Ah, Rome! Well, well; I made thee miserable
　　What time° I threw the people's suffrages
　　On him that thus doth tyrannize o'er me.　　　　*20*
　　Go, get you gone, and pray be careful all,
　　And leave you not a man of war unsearched:
　　This wicked emperor may have shipped her hence,
　　And, kinsmen, then we may go pipe for° justice.

Marcus. O, Publius, is not this a heavy case,　　　*25*

IV.iii.3 *home* fully　4 *Terras Astraea reliquit* Astraea (goddess of
justice) has left the earth (Latin; from Ovid, *Metamorphoses*, I.150)
5 *Be you rememb'red* remember　8 *Happily* perhaps　13 *Pluto's
region* Hades　19 *What time* when　24 *pipe for* i.e., whistle vainly
for

To see thy noble uncle thus distract?

Publius. Therefore, my lords, it highly us concerns
    By day and night t' attend him carefully,
    And feed his humor° kindly as we may,
30   Till time beget some careful remedy.

Marcus. Kinsmen, his sorrows are past remedy.
    But° . . .
    Join with the Goths, and with revengeful war
    Take wreak° on Rome for this ingratitude,
35   And vengeance on the traitor Saturnine.

Titus. Publius, how now! How now, my masters!
    What, have you met with her?

Publius. No, my good lord, but Pluto sends you word,
    If you will have revenge from hell, you shall:
40   Marry, for Justice, she is so employed,
    He thinks, with Jove in heaven, or somewhere else,
    So that perforce you must needs stay a time.

Titus. He doth me wrong to feed me with delays.
    I'll dive into the burning lake below,
45   And pull her out of Acheron° by the heels.
    Marcus, we are but shrubs, no cedars we,
    No big-boned men framed of the Cyclops'° size;
    But metal, Marcus, steel to the very back,
    Yet wrung with wrongs more than our backs can
        bear:
50   And sith° there's no justice in earth nor hell,
    We will solicit heaven, and move the gods
    To send down Justice for to wreak° our wrongs.
    Come, to this gear.° You are a good archer, Marcus.
                   He gives them the arrows.
    Ad Jovem, that's for you: here, *Ad Apollinem:*
55   *Ad Martem,*° that's for myself:

29 *humor* mood, caprice 32 *But* (a catchword indicates that the
line begins "But," though the line itself was omitted) 34 *wreak*
vengeance 45 *Acheron* river in Hades 47 *Cyclops* giants (in
Homer's *Odyssey*) 50 *sith* since 52 *wreak* avenge 53 *gear* affair
54–55 *Ad Jovem . . . Ad Apollinem:/Ad Martem* to Jove . . . to
Apollo; to Mars (Latin)

Here, boy, to Pallas: here, to Mercury:
To Saturn, Caius, not to Saturnine;
You were as good to shoot° against the wind.
To it, boy! Marcus, loose when I bid.
Of my word, I have written to effect;   60
There's not a god left unsolicited.

Marcus. Kinsmen, shoot all your shafts into the court:
We will afflict the Emperor in his pride.

Titus. Now, masters, draw. O, well said, Lucius!
Good boy, in Virgo's° lap; give it Pallas.   65

Marcus. My lord, I aim a mile beyond the moon;
Your letter is with Jupiter by this.

Titus. Ha, ha!
Publius, Publius, what hast thou done!
See, see, thou hast shot off one of Taurus' horns.   70

Marcus. This was the sport, my lord: when Publius
    shot,
The bull being galled, gave Aries such a knock
That down fell both the Ram's horns in the court,
And who should find them but the Empress' villain?
She laughed, and told the Moor he should not
    choose   75
But give them to his master for a present.

Titus. Why, there it goes! God give his lordship joy!

Enter the Clown,° with a basket and two pigeons in it.

News, news from heaven! Marcus, the post is come.
Sirrah, what tidings? Have you any letters?
Shall I have justice? What says Jupiter?   80

Clown. Ho, the gibbet maker!° He says that he hath

58 *You were as good to shoot* you would do as much good by shooting   65 *Virgo's* the Virgin's (sign of the zodiac, as are *Taurus*—the
bull—in line 70, and *Aries*—the ram—in line 72)   77 s.d. *Clown*
rustic fellow   81 *gibbet maker* (apparently "Jupiter"—which in the
original text is spelled "Jubiter"—was pronounced rather like "gib-
beter," i.e., gibbet maker)

taken them down again, for the man must not be
hanged till the next week.

Titus. But what says Jupiter, I ask thee?

85　*Clown.* Alas, sir, I know not Jubiter; I never drank
with him in all my life.

Titus. Why, villain, art not thou the carrier?

Clown. Ay, of my pigeons, sir, nothing else.

Titus. Why, didst thou not come from heaven?

90　*Clown.* From heaven? Alas, sir, I never came there!
God forbid, I should be so bold to press to heaven
in my young days. Why, I am going with my
pigeons to the tribunal plebs,° to take up a matter
of brawl betwixt my uncle and one of the Emperal's
95　men.

Marcus. Why, sir, that is as fit as can be to serve for
your oration; and let him deliver the pigeons to the
Emperor from you.

Titus. Tell me, can you deliver an oration to the
100　Emperor with a grace?

Clown. Nay, truly, sir, I could never say grace in all
my life.

Titus. Sirrah, come hither: make no more ado,
But give your pigeons to the Emperor:
105　By me thou shalt have justice at his hands.
Hold, hold, meanwhile, here's money for thy
charges.°
Give me pen and ink. Sirrah, can you with a grace
deliver up a supplication?

Clown. Ay, sir.

110　*Titus.* Then here is a supplication for you. And when
you come to him, at the first approach you must

93 *tribunal plebs* (malaprop for *tribunus plebis,* "Tribune of the
plebs"; *Emperal,* later in the sentence, is another malaprop)　106
charges i.e., pigeons

kneel, then kiss his foot, then deliver up your
pigeons, and then look for your reward. I'll be at
hand, sir! See you do it bravely.°

Clown. I warrant you, sir, let me alone.   115

Titus. Sirrah, hast thou a knife? Come, let me see it.
Here, Marcus, fold it in the oration,
For thou hast made it like an humble suppliant.
And when thou hast given it to the Emperor,
Knock at my door, and tell me what he says.   120

Clown. God be with you, sir; I will.   *Exit.*

Titus. Come, Marcus, let us go. Publius, follow me.
                                            Exeunt.

[Scene IV. *Rome. Before the palace.*]

*Enter Emperor and Empress and her two sons.
The Emperor brings the arrows in his hand that
Titus shot at him.*

Saturninus. Why, lords, what wrongs are these! Was
          ever seen
An emperor in Rome thus overborne,
Troubled, confronted thus, and for the extent°
Of egal° justice used in such contempt?
My lords, you know, as know the mightful gods,   5
However these disturbers of our peace
Buzz in the people's ears, there naught hath passed
But even° with law against the willful sons
Of old Andronicus. And what and if
His sorrows have so overwhelmed his wits,   10
Shall we be thus afflicted in his wreaks,°
His fits, his frenzy, and his bitterness?

114 *bravely* well   IV.iv.3 *extent* exercise   4 *egal* equal   8 *even*
agreeing   11 *wreaks* vengeful acts

And now he writes to heaven for his redress!
See, here's to Jove, and this to Mercury,
15 This to Apollo, this to the god of war.
Sweet scrolls to fly about the streets of Rome!
What's this but libeling against the Senate,
And blazoning° our unjustice everywhere?
A goodly humor, is it not, my lords?
20 As who would say, in Rome no justice were.
But if I live, his feignèd ecstasies°
Shall be no shelter to these outrages,
But he and his shall know that justice lives
In Saturninus' health; whom, if he sleep,
25 He'll so awake, as he in fury shall
Cut off the proud'st conspirator that lives.

Tamora. My gracious lord, my lovely Saturnine,
Lord of my life, commander of my thoughts,
Calm thee, and bear the faults of Titus' age,
30 Th' effects of sorrow for his valiant sons,
Whose loss hath pierced him deep and scarred his
      heart,
And rather comfort his distressèd plight
Than prosecute the meanest or the best
For these contempts. [*Aside*] Why, thus it shall
      become
35 High-witted Tamora to gloze° with all.
But, Titus, I have touched thee to the quick,
Thy lifeblood out:° if Aaron now be wise,
Then is all safe, the anchor in the port.

Enter Clown.

How now, good fellow? Wouldst thou speak with
us?

40 *Clown.* Yea, forsooth, and your mistress-ship be em-
perial.

Tamora. Empress I am, but yonder sits the Emperor.

Clown. 'Tis he. God and Saint Stephen give you

18 *blazoning* proclaiming   21 *ecstasies* fits of madness   35 *gloze* use
specious words   37 *Thy lifeblood out* when your blood is out

godden.° I have brought you a letter and a couple
of pigeons here.   45

    He [i.e., Saturninus] reads the letter.

Saturninus. Go, take him away, and hang him presently.

Clown. How much money must I have?

Tamora. Come, sirrah, you must be hanged.

Clown. Hanged! By lady,° then I have brought up a
  neck° to a fair end.   *Exit [with guards].*   50

Saturninus. Despiteful and intolerable wrongs!
  Shall I endure this monstrous villainy?
  I know from whence this same device proceeds.
  May this be borne as if his traitorous sons,
  That died by law for murder of our brother,   55
  Have by my means been butchered wrongfully.
  Go, drag the villain hither by the hair,
  Nor age nor honor shall shape privilege:°
  For this proud mock I'll be thy slaughter-man—
  Sly frantic wretch, that holp'st to make me great,   60
  In hope thyself should govern Rome and me.

    Enter nuntius,° Aemilius.

What news with thee, Aemilius?

Aemilius. Arm, my lords. Rome never had more
  cause.
  The Goths have gathered head,° and with a power°
  Of high-resolvèd men, bent to the spoil,   65
  They hither march amain, under conduct°
  Of Lucius, son to old Andronicus;
  Who threats, in course of this revenge, to do
  As much as ever Coriolanus° did.

44 *godden* good evening   49 *By lady* (an interjection, from "By
Our Lady")   50 *neck* (possibly with a pun on "knack," which means
"deceitful trick")   58 *shape privilege* provide immunity   61 s.d.
nuntius messenger (Latin)   64 *gathered head* raised an army   64
power army   66 *conduct* leadership   69 *Coriolanus* (this Roman
hero who became Rome's enemy is the protagonist in Shakespeare's
last tragedy)

70 *Saturninus.* Is warlike Lucius general of the Goths?
These tidings nip me, and I hang the head
As flowers with frost or grass beat down with
storms.
Ay, now begins our sorrows to approach:
'Tis he the common people love so much;
75 Myself hath often heard them say,
When I have walkèd like a private man,
That Lucius' banishment was wrongfully,
And they have wished that Lucius were their
emperor.

Tamora. Why should you fear? Is not your city
strong?

80 *Saturninus.* Ay, but the citizens favor Lucius,
And will revolt from me to succor him.

Tamora. King, be thy thoughts imperious, like thy
name.
Is the sun dimmed, that gnats do fly in it?
The eagle suffers little birds to sing
85 And is not careful° what they mean thereby,
Knowing that with the shadow of his wings
He can at pleasure stint° their melody:
Even so mayst thou the giddy men of Rome.
Then cheer thy spirit: for know, thou Emperor,
90 I will enchant the old Andronicus
With words more sweet, and yet more dangerous,
Than baits to fish, or honey-stalks° to sheep;
Whenas the one is wounded with the bait,
The other rotted with delicious feed.

95 *Saturninus.* But he will not entreat his son for us.

Tamora. If Tamora entreat him, then he will:
For I can smooth, and fill his agèd ears
With golden promises, that, were his heart
Almost impregnable, his old ears deaf,
100 Yet should both ear and heart obey my tongue.

85 *careful* worried   87 *stint* stop   92 *honey-stalks* clover

[*To Aemilius*] Go thou before to be our ambassa-
    dor:
Say that the Emperor requests a parley
Of warlike Lucius, and appoint the meeting
Even at his father's house, the old Andronicus.

Saturninus. Aemilius, do this message honorably,   *105*
    And if he stand in° hostage for his safety,
    Bid him demand what pledge will please him best.

Aemilius. Your bidding shall I do effectually.   *Exit.*

Tamora. Now will I to that old Andronicus,
    And temper° him with all the art I have,   *110*
    To pluck proud Lucius from the warlike Goths.
    And now, sweet Emperor, be blithe again,
    And bury all thy fear in my devices.

Saturninus. Then go successantly,° and plead to him.

                                        Exeunt.

---

106 *stand in* insist upon   110 *temper* work upon   114 *successantly*
one after the other(?)

[ACT V

Scene I. *A plain near Rome.*]

Enter Lucius, with an army of Goths, with drums and soldiers.

Lucius. Approvèd° warriors, and my faithful friends,
I have receivèd letters from great Rome,
Which signifies what hate they bear their emperor,
And how desirous of our sight they are.
5 Therefore, great lords, be, as your titles witness,
Imperious, and impatient of your wrongs;
And wherein Rome hath done you any scath,°
Let him make treble satisfaction.

Goth. Brave slip,° sprung from the great Andronicus,
10 Whose name was once our terror, now our comfort,
Whose high exploits and honorable deeds
Ingrateful Rome requites with foul contempt,
Be bold° in us: we'll follow where thou lead'st,
Like stinging bees in hottest summer's day,
15 Led by their master to the flow'red fields,
And be advengèd on cursèd Tamora.

[*Other Goths.*] And as he saith, so say we all with him.

Lucius. I humbly thank him, and I thank you all.
But who comes here, led by a lusty Goth?

V.i.1 *Approvèd* tested   7 *scath* harm   9 *slip* offshoot   13 *bold* confident

*Enter a Goth, leading of Aaron with his child
in his arms.*

Goth. Renownèd Lucius, from our troops I strayed   20
 To gaze upon a ruinous monastery,
 And, as I earnestly did fix mine eye
 Upon the wasted° building, suddenly
 I heard a child cry underneath a wall.
 I made unto the noise, when soon I heard   25
 The crying babe controlled with this discourse:
 "Peace, tawny° slave, half me and half thy dame,
 Did not thy hue bewray° whose brat° thou art,
 Had nature lent thee but thy mother's look,
 Villain, thou mightst have been an emperor: 30
 But where the bull and cow are both milk-white,
 They never do beget a coal-black calf.
 Peace, villain, peace!" Even thus he rates° the
  babe,
 "For I must bear thee to a trusty Goth,
 Who, when he knows thou art the Empress' babe,   35
 Will hold thee dearly for thy mother's sake."
 With this, my weapon drawn, I rushed upon him,
 Surprised him suddenly, and brought him hither,
 To use as you think needful of the man.

Lucius. O worthy Goth, this is the incarnate devil   40
 That robbed Andronicus of his good hand.
 This is the pearl that pleased your empress' eye,
 And here's the base fruit of her burning lust.
 Say, wall-eyed° slave, whither wouldst thou convey
 This growing image of thy fiendlike face?   45
 Why dost not speak? What, deaf? Not a word?
 A halter, soldiers! Hang him on this tree,
 And by his side his fruit of bastardy.

Aaron. Touch not the boy; he is of royal blood.

Lucius. Too like the sire for ever being good.   50
 First hang the child, that he may see it sprawl—

---

23 *wasted* ruined 27 *tawny* black 27 *dame* mother 28 *bewray*
reveal 28 *brat* young offspring 33 *rates* berates 44 *wall-eyed*
glaring (literally: having a whitish iris)

A sight to vex the father's soul withal.

Aaron. Get me a ladder.° Lucius, save the child,
And bear it from me to the Empress.
₅₅ If thou do this, I'll show thee wondrous things
That highly may advantage thee to hear.
If thou wilt not, befall what may befall,
I'll speak no more but "Vengeance rot you all!"

Lucius. Say on, and if it please me which thou
speak'st,
₆₀ Thy child shall live, and I will see it nourished.

Aaron. And if it please thee! Why, assure thee,
Lucius,
'Twill vex thy soul to hear what I shall speak;
For I must talk of murders, rapes, and massacres,
Acts of black night, abominable deeds,
₆₅ Complots of mischief, treason, villainies
Ruthful° to hear, yet piteously performed:°
And this shall all be buried in my death,
Unless thou swear to me my child shall live.

Lucius. Tell on thy mind, I say thy child shall live.

₇₀ *Aaron.* Swear that he shall, and then I will begin.

Lucius. Who should I swear by? Thou believest no
god:
That granted, how canst thou believe an oath?

Aaron. What if I do not? As indeed I do not;
Yet, for I know thou art religious,
₇₅ And hast a thing within thee callèd conscience,
With twenty popish tricks and ceremonies,
Which I have seen thee careful to observe,
Therefore I urge thy oath; for that I know
An idiot holds his bauble° for a god,
₈₀ And keeps the oath which by that god he swears,
To that I'll urge him: therefore thou shalt vow
By that same god, what god soe'er it be,

53 *Get me a ladder* i.e., hang me rather than the child   66 *Ruthful*
pitiful   66 *piteously performed* i.e., performed, which excites pity
79 *bauble* carved head at the end of a court fool's stick

That thou adorest and hast in reverence,
To save my boy, to nourish and bring him up;
Or else I will discover naught to thee.   85

Lucius. Even by my god I swear to thee I will.

Aaron. First know thou, I begot him on the Empress.

Lucius. O most insatiate and luxurious° woman!

Aaron. Tut, Lucius, this was but a deed of charity
To° that which thou shalt hear of me anon.   90
'Twas her two sons that murdered Bassianus;
They cut thy sister's tongue and ravished her,
And cut her hands, and trimmed her as thou sawest.

Lucius. O detestable villain! Call'st thou that trim-
ming?

Aaron. Why, she was washed, and cut, and trimmed,
and 'twas   95
Trim sport for them which had the doing of it.

Lucius. O barbarous, beastly villains, like thyself!

Aaron. Indeed, I was their tutor to instruct them.
That codding° spirit had they from their mother,
As sure a card as ever won the set.°
That bloody mind, I think, they learned of me,   100
As true a dog as ever fought at head.°
Well, let my deeds be witness of my worth.
I trained° thy brethren to that guileful hole,
Where the dead corpse of Bassianus lay;
I wrote the letter that thy father found,   105
And hid the gold within that letter mentioned,
Confederate with the Queen and her two sons;
And what not done, that thou hast cause to rue,
Wherein I had no stroke of mischief in it?   110
I played the cheater° for thy father's hand,
And when I had it drew myself apart,

---

88 *luxurious* lustful   90   *To* in comparison with   99 *codding* lustful   100 *set* game   102 *at head* (a courageous bulldog went for
the bull's nose)   104 *trained* lured   111 *cheater* officer appointed
to look after escheats or property forfeited to the Crown

And almost broke my heart with extreme laughter.
I pried me through the crevice of a wall,
115 When for his hand he had his two sons' heads;
Beheld his tears and laughed so heartily
That both mine eyes were rainy like to his:
And when I told the Empress of this sport,
She sounded° almost at my pleasing tale,
120 And for my tidings gave me twenty kisses.

Goth. What, canst thou say all this and never blush?

Aaron. Ay, like a black dog, as the saying is.

Lucius. Art thou not sorry for these heinous deeds?

Aaron. Ay, that I had not done a thousand more.
125 Even now I curse the day—and yet, I think,
Few come within the compass of my curse—
Wherein I did not some notorious ill:
As kill a man or else devise his death,
Ravish a maid or plot the way to do it,
130 Accuse some innocent and forswear° myself,
Set deadly enmity between two friends,
Make poor men's cattle break their necks,
Set fire on barns and haystalks in the night,
And bid the owners quench them with their tears.
135 Oft have I digged up dead men from their graves
And set them upright at their dear friends' door,
Even when their sorrows almost was forgot,
And on their skins, as on the bark of trees,
Have with my knife carvèd in Roman letters,
140 "Let not your sorrow die, though I am dead."
But, I have done a thousand dreadful things
As willingly as one would kill a fly,
And nothing grieves me heartily indeed,
But that I cannot do ten thousand more.

145 *Lucius.* Bring down the devil, for he must not die
So sweet a death as hanging presently.

Aaron. If there be devils, would I were a devil,
To live and burn in everlasting fire,

119 *sounded* swooned   130 *forswear* perjure

So I might have your company in hell,
But to torment you with my bitter tongue!   *150*

Lucius. Sirs, stop his mouth, and let him speak no
  more.
                    Enter Aemilius.

Goth. My lord, there is a messenger from Rome   *155*
  Desires to be admitted to your presence.

Lucius. Let him come near.
  Welcome, Aemilius, what's the news from Rome?

Aemilius. Lord Lucius, and you princes of the Goths,
  The Roman Emperor greets you all by me;
  And, for he understands you are in arms,
  He craves a parley at your father's house,
  Willing you to demand your hostages,   *160*
  And they shall be immediately delivered.

Goth. What says our general?

Lucius. Aemilius, let the Emperor give his pledges
  Unto my father and my uncle Marcus,
  And we will come. March away.   [*Exeunt.*]   *165*

[Scene II. *Rome. Before Titus' house.*]

Enter Tamora and her two sons, disguised [*as
  Revenge attended by Rape and Murder*].

Tamora. Thus, in this strange and sad habiliment,°
  I will encounter with Andronicus,
  And say I am Revenge, sent from below
  To join with him and right his heinous wrongs.
  Knock at his study, where, they say, he keeps°   *5*
  To ruminate strange plots of dire revenge;
  Tell him Revenge is come to join with him,
  And work confusion° on his enemies.

V.ii.1 *sad habiliment* dismal apparel 5 *keeps* dwells 8 *confusion*
destruction

They knock, and Titus [above] opens his study door.

Titus. Who doth molest my contemplation?
10 Is it your trick to make me ope the door,
    That so my sad decrees may fly away,
    And all my study be to no effect?
    You are deceived: for what I mean to do
    See here in bloody lines I have set down.
15 And what is written shall be executed.

Tamora. Titus, I am come to talk with thee.

Titus. No, not a word. How can I grace my talk,
    Wanting a hand to give that accord?°
    Thou hast the odds of° me, therefore no more.

Tamora. If thou didst know me, thou wouldst talk
20   with me.

Titus. I am not mad, I know thee well enough.
    Witness this wretched stump, witness these crimson
        lines,
    Witness these trenches made by grief and care,
    Witness the tiring day and heavy night,
25 Witness all sorrow, that I know thee well
    For our proud empress, mighty Tamora:
    Is not thy coming for my other hand?

Tamora. Know thou, sad man, I am not Tamora;
    She is thy enemy, and I thy friend.
30 I am Revenge, sent from th' infernal kingdom
    To ease the gnawing vulture of thy mind,
    By working wreakful° vengeance on thy foes.
    Come down and welcome me to this world's light;
    Confer with me of murder and of death:
35 There's not a hollow cave or lurking place,
    No vast obscurity or misty vale,
    Where bloody murder or detested rape
    Can couch° for fear, but I will find them out,

---

18 *give that accord* i.e., provide appropriate gestures 19 *odds of*
advantage over 32 *wreakful* avenging 38 *couch* lie hidden

   And in their ears tell them my dreadful name,
   Revenge, which makes the foul offender quake.   40

Titus. Art thou Revenge? And art thou sent to me,
   To be a torment to mine enemies?

Tamora. I am, therefore come down and welcome me.

Titus. Do me some service ere I come to thee.
   Lo, by thy side where Rape and Murder stands;   45
   Now give some surance° that thou art Revenge;
   Stab them, or tear them on thy chariot wheels;
   And then I'll come and be thy wagoner,
   And whirl along with thee about the globes.
   Provide thee two proper palfreys,° black as jet,   50
   To hale thy vengeful wagon swift away,
   And find out murder in their guilty caves:
   And when thy car° is loaden with their heads,
   I will dismount, and by thy wagon wheel
   Trot like a servile footman all day long,   55
   Even from Hyperion's° rising in the east,
   Until his very downfall in the sea.
   And day by day I'll do this heavy task,
   So° thou destroy Rapine° and Murder there.

Tamora. These are my ministers and come with me.   60

Titus. Are them thy ministers? What are they called?

Tamora. Rape and Murder; therefore callèd so,
   'Cause they take vengeance of such kind of men.

Titus. Good Lord, how like the Empress' sons they are!
   And you the Empress! But we worldly° men   65
   Have miserable, mad, mistaking eyes.
   O sweet Revenge, now do I come to thee:
   And, if one arm's embracement will content thee,
   I will embrace thee in it by and by. [*Exit above.*]

Tamora. This closing° with him fits his lunacy.   70

---

46 *surance* assurance   50 *proper palfreys* excellent horses   53 *car*
chariot   56 *Hyperion's* the sun god's   59 *So* provided that   59
Rapine rape   65 *worldly* mortal, of this world   70 *closing* agreement

Whate'er I forge° to feed his brainsick humors,
Do you uphold and maintain in your speeches,
For now he firmly takes me for Revenge,
And, being credulous in this mad thought,
75   I'll make him send for Lucius his son;
And, whilst I at a banket hold him sure,
I'll find some cunning practice° out of hand,°
To scatter and disperse the giddy Goths,
Or at the least make them his enemies.
80   See, here he comes, and I must ply my theme.

[*Enter Titus.*]

Titus. Long have I been forlorn, and all for thee.
Welcome, dread Fury, to my woeful house:
Rapine and Murder, you are welcome too:
How like the Empress and her sons you are!
85   Well are you fitted, had you but a Moor:
Could not all hell afford you such a devil?
For well I wot the Empress never wags°
But in her company there is a Moor;
And, would you represent our queen aright,
90   It were convenient° you had such a devil:
But welcome, as you are. What shall we do?

Tamora. What wouldst thou have us do, Andronicus?

Demetrius. Show me a murderer, I'll deal with him.

Chiron. Show me a villain that hath done a rape,
95   And I am sent to be revengèd on him.

Tamora. Show me a thousand that hath done thee
     wrong,
And I will be revengèd on them all.

Titus. Look round about the wicked streets of Rome,
And when thou find'st a man that's like thyself,
100   Good Murder, stab him; he's a murderer.
Go thou with him, and when it is thy hap°
To find another that is like to thee,

71 *forge* invent   77 *practice* scheme   77 *out of hand* on the spur
of the moment   87 *wags* moves   90 *convenient* fitting   101 *hap*
chance

Good Rapine, stab him; he is a ravisher.
Go thou with them, and in the Emperor's court
There is a queen attended by a Moor;   105
Well shalt thou know her by thine own proportion,
For up and down she doth resemble thee;
I pray thee, do on them some violent death;
They have been violent to me and mine.

Tamora. Well hast thou lessoned us; this shall we do. 110
But would it please thee, good Andronicus,
To send for Lucius, thy thrice valiant son,
Who leads towards Rome a band of warlike Goths,
And bid him come and banquet at thy house:
When he is here, even at thy solemn° feast,   115
I will bring in the Empress and her sons,
The Emperor himself, and all thy foes,
And at thy mercy shall they stoop and kneel,
And on them shalt thou ease thy angry heart.
What says Andronicus to this device?   120

Titus. Marcus, my brother! 'Tis sad Titus calls.

Enter Marcus.

Go, gentle Marcus, to thy nephew Lucius;
Thou shalt inquire him out among the Goths.
Bid him repair° to me and bring with him
Some of the chiefest princes of the Goths: 125
Bid him encamp his soldiers where they are;
Tell him the Emperor and the Empress too
Feast at my house, and he shall feast with them.
This do thou for my love, and so let him,
As he regards his agèd father's life.   130

Marcus. This will I do, and soon return again. [*Exit.*]

Tamora. Now will I hence about thy business,
And take my ministers along with me.

Titus. Nay, nay, let Rape and Murder stay with me,
Or else I'll call my brother back again,   135
And cleave to no revenge but Lucius.

115 *solemn* ceremonious   124 *repair* come

Tamora. [*Aside to her sons*] What say you, boys? Will
    you abide with him,
    Whiles I go tell my lord the Emperor
    How I have governed our determined jest?°
140   Yield to his humor, smooth and speak him fair,°
    And tarry with him till I turn again.

Titus. [*Aside*] I knew them all, though they supposed
    me mad;
    And will o'erreach them in their own devices,
    A pair of cursèd hellhounds and their dame.

145 *Demetrius.* Madam, depart at pleasure, leave us here.

Tamora. Farewell, Andronicus: Revenge now goes
    To lay a complot° to betray thy foes.

Titus. I know thou dost; and, sweet Revenge, farewell.
                    [*Exit Tamora.*]

Chiron. Tell us, old man, how shall we be employed?

150 *Titus.* Tut, I have work enough for you to do.
    Publius, come hither, Caius, and Valentine!

         [*Enter Publius and others.*]

Publius. What is your will?

Titus. Know you these two?

Publius. The Empress' sons, I take them: Chiron,
155   Demetrius.

Titus. Fie, Publius, fie! Thou art too much deceived;
    The one is Murder, and Rape is the other's name:
    And therefore bind them, gentle Publius:
    Caius and Valentine, lay hands on them:
160   Oft have you heard me wish for such an hour,
    And now I find it: therefore bind them sure;
    And stop their mouths if they begin to cry. [*Exit.*]

---

139 *governed our determined jest* managed the jest we agreed ("determined") upon   140 *smooth and speak him fair* flatter and speak
courteously to him   147 *complot* plot

Chiron. Villains, forbear! We are the Empress' sons.

Publius. And therefore do we what we are commanded.
   Stop close their mouths, let them not speak a word: 165
   Is he sure bound? Look that you bind them fast.

*Enter Titus Andronicus with a knife, and Lavinia with
a basin.*

Titus. Come, come, Lavinia; look, thy foes are bound.
   Sirs, stop their mouths, let them not speak to me,
   But let them hear what fearful words I utter.
   O villains, Chiron and Demetrius!   170
   Here stands the spring whom you have stained with
      mud,
   This goodly summer with your winter mixed.
   You killed her husband, and, for that vile fault
   Two of her brothers were condemned to death,
   My hand cut off and made a merry jest: 175
   Both her sweet hands, her tongue, and that more dear
   Than hands or tongue, her spotless chastity,
   Inhuman traitors, you constrained and forced.
   What would you say if I should let you speak?
   Villains, for shame you could not beg for grace.   180
   Hark, wretches, how I mean to martyr you.
   This one hand yet is left to cut your throats,
   Whiles that Lavinia 'tween her stumps doth hold
   The basin that receives your guilty blood.
   You know your mother means to feast with me,   185
   And calls herself Revenge, and thinks me mad:
   Hark, villains, I will grind your bones to dust,
   And with your blood and it I'll make a paste,
   And of the paste a coffin° I will rear,
   And make two pasties of your shameful heads,   190
   And bid that strumpet, your unhallowed dam,
   Like to the earth, swallow her own increase.°
   This is the feast that I have bid her to,
   And this the banket she shall surfeit on;
   For worse than Philomel you used my daughter,   195

189 *coffin* pie crust   192 *increase* offspring

And worse than Progne° I will be revenged.
And now prepare your throats. Lavinia, come,
Receive the blood; and when that they are dead,
Let me go grind their bones to powder small,
200   And with this hateful liquor temper° it,
And in that paste let their vile heads be baked.
Come, come, be every one officious°
To make this banket, which I wish may prove
More stern and bloody than the Centaurs' feast.°
                                        He cuts their throats.
205   So, now bring them in, for I'll play the cook,
And see them ready against° their mother comes.
                                        Exeunt.

[Scene III. *Rome. Within Titus' house.*]

*Enter Lucius, Marcus, and the Goths [with Aaron a
prisoner, and an Attendant bearing Aaron's child].*

Lucius. Uncle Marcus, since 'tis my father's mind
That I repair° to Rome, I am content.

Goth. And ours with thine, befall what fortune will.

Lucius. Good uncle, take you in this barbarous Moor,
5   This ravenous tiger, this accursèd devil;
Let him receive no sust'nance, fetter him,
Till he be brought unto the Empress' face
For testimony of her foul proceedings:
And see the ambush of our friends be strong;
10   I fear the Emperor means no good to us.

196 *Progne* wife of Tereus (Tereus raped and mutilated Progne's
sister, Philomela, and in revenge Progne slaughtered Tereus'—and
her own—son and served him to Tereus) 200 *temper* mix 202
officious busy 204 *Centaurs' feast* (a battle followed the marriage
feast to which the Lapiths invited the Centaurs) 206 *against* in
preparation for the time when V.iii.2 *repair* return

Aaron. Some devil whisper curses in my ear,
   And prompt me, that my tongue may utter forth
   The venomous malice of my swelling heart!

Lucius. Away, inhuman dog! Unhallowed slave!
   Sirs, help our uncle to convey him in.   15
              [*Goths lead Aaron in. Trumpets sound.*]
   The trumpets show the Emperor is at hand.

*Sound trumpets. Enter Emperor and Empress, with
          Tribunes and others.*

Saturninus. What, hath the firmament mo° suns than
   one?

Lucius. What boots° it thee to call thyself a sun?

Marcus. Rome's Emperor, and nephew, break the
   parle;°
   These quarrels must be quietly debated.   20
   The feast is ready, which the careful° Titus
   Hath ordained to an honorable end,
   For peace, for love, for league, and good to Rome.
   Please you, therefore, draw nigh, and take your
     places.

Saturninus. Marcus, we will.   25

*Trumpets sounding, enter Titus, like a cook,
placing the dishes, and Lavinia with a veil over
   her face, [young Lucius, and others].*

Titus. Welcome, my lord; welcome, dread Queen;
   Welcome, ye warlike Goths; welcome, Lucius;
   And welcome, all: although the cheer° be poor,
   'Twill fill your stomachs; please you eat of it.

Saturninus. Why art thou thus attired, Andronicus?   30

Titus. Because I would be sure to have all well,
   To entertain your Highness and your empress.

Tamora. We are beholding to you, good Andronicus.

17 *mo* more   18 *boots* avails   19 *break the parle* interrupt the talk
(i.e., cease quarreling)   21 *careful* full of sorrow   28 *cheer* hos-
pitality

Titus. And if your Highness knew my heart, you were.
35   My lord the Emperor, resolve° me this:
  Was it well done of rash Virginius
  To slay his daughter with his own right hand,
  Because she was enforced,° stained, and deflow'r'd?

Saturninus. It was, Andronicus.

40 *Titus.* Your reason, mighty lord!

Saturninus. Because the girl should not survive her
    shame,
  And by her presence still renew his sorrows.

Titus. A reason mighty, strong, and effectual,
  A pattern, precedent, and lively warrant,
45   For me, most wretched, to perform the like.
  Die, die, Lavinia, and thy shame with thee,
  And with thy shame thy father's sorrow die!
                              [*He kills her.*]

Saturninus. What hast thou done, unnatural and un-
    kind?°

Titus. Killed her for whom my tears have made me
    blind.
50   I am as woeful as Virginius was,
  And have a thousand times more cause than he
  To do this outrage, and it now is done.

Saturninus. What, was she ravished? Tell who did the
    deed.

Titus. Will't please you eat? Will't please your Highness
    feed?

55 *Tamora.* Why hast thou slain thine only daughter thus?

Titus. Not I; 'twas Chiron and Demetrius:
  They ravished her and cut away her tongue;
  And they, 'twas they, that did her all this wrong.

Saturninus. Go, fetch them hither to us presently.

---

35 *resolve* answer   38 *enforced* forced, raped   48 *unkind* (1) unnatural (2) cruel

Titus. Why, there they are, both bakèd in this pie,   60
　Whereof their mother daintily hath fed,
　Eating the flesh that she herself hath bred.
　'Tis true, 'tis true; witness my knife's sharp point.
　　　　　　　　　He stabs the Empress.

Saturninus. Die, frantic wretch, for this accursèd deed.
　　　　　　　　　[*Kills Titus.*]

Lucius. Can the son's eye behold his father bleed?   65
　There's meed for meed,° death for a deadly deed.
　　　　　　　　　[*Kills Saturninus.*]

Marcus. You sad-faced men, people and sons of Rome,
　By uproars severed, as a flight of fowl
　Scattered by winds and high tempestuous gusts,
　O, let me teach you how to knit again   70
　This scattered corn into one mutual sheaf,
　These broken limbs again into one body.

Roman Lord. Let Rome herself be bane° unto herself,
　And she whom mighty kingdoms curtsy to,
　Like a forlorn and desperate castaway,   75
　Do shameful execution on herself,
　But if° my frosty signs and chaps of age,°
　Grave witnesses of true experience,
　Cannot induce you to attend my words.
　[*To Lucius*] Speak, Rome's dear friend, as erst°
　　our ancestor,°   80
　When with his solemn tongue he did discourse
　To lovesick Dido's sad attending° ear
　The story of that baleful° burning night,
　When subtle Greeks surprised King Priam's Troy;
　Tell us what Sinon° hath bewitched our ears,   85
　Or who hath brought the fatal engine in
　That gives our Troy, our Rome, the civil wound.
　My heart is not compact° of flint nor steel;

66 *meed for meed* measure for measure   73 *bane* destruction   77
But if unless   77 *frosty signs and chaps of age* i.e., white hair and
cracked (wrinkled) skin   80 *erst* formerly   80 *our ancestor* i.e.,
Aeneas   82 *sad attending* seriously listening   83 *baleful* injurious
85 *Sinon* Greek who persuaded the Trojans to admit the wooden
horse   88 *compact* composed

Nor can I utter all our bitter grief,
90   But floods of tears will drown my oratory
And break my utt'rance, even in the time
When it should move ye to attend me most,
And force you to commiseration.
Here's Rome's young captain, let him tell the tale,
95   While I stand by and weep to hear him speak.

Lucius. Then, gracious auditory, be it known to you
That Chiron and the damned Demetrius
Were they that murd'red our emperor's brother;
And they it were that ravishèd our sister.
100   For their fell° faults our brothers were beheaded,
Our father's tears despised, and basely cozened°
Of that true hand that fought Rome's quarrel out
And sent her enemies unto the grave.
Lastly, myself unkindly banishèd,
105   The gates shut on me, and turned weeping out,
To beg relief among Rome's enemies,
Who drowned their enmity in my true tears
And oped their arms to embrace me as a friend:
I am the turned-forth, be it known to you,
110   That have preserved her welfare in my blood,
And from her bosom took the enemy's point,
Sheathing the steel in my advent'rous body.
Alas, you know I am no vaunter,° I;
My scars can witness, dumb although they are,
115   That my report is just and full of truth.
But, soft!° Methinks, I do digress too much,
Citing my worthless praise. O, pardon me,
For when no friends are by, men praise themselves.

Marcus. Now is my turn to speak. Behold the child:
120   Of this was Tamora deliverèd,
The issue of an irreligious Moor,
Chief architect and plotter of these woes:
The villain is alive in Titus' house,
And as he is to witness, this is true.
125   Now judge what cause had Titus to revenge

100 *fell* savage   101 *cozened* cheated   113 *vaunter* braggart   116
soft hold (a common interjection)

These wrongs, unspeakable, past patience,
Or more than any living man could bear.
Now have you heard the truth. What say you,
    Romans?
Have we done aught amiss, show us wherein,
And, from the place where you behold us pleading,   130
The poor remainder of Andronici
Will, hand in hand, all headlong hurl ourselves
And on the ragged° stones beat forth our souls,
And make a mutual closure° of our house.
Speak, Romans, speak, and if you say we shall,   135
Lo, hand in hand, Lucius and I will fall.

Aemilius. Come, come, thou reverend man of Rome,
And bring our emperor gently in thy hand,
Lucius our emperor; for well I know
The common voice do cry it shall be so.   140

Marcus. Lucius, all hail, Rome's royal Emperor!
[*To soldiers*] Go, go into old Titus' sorrowful
    house,
And hither hale that misbelieving Moor,
To be adjudged some direful slaught'ring death,
As punishment for his most wicked life.   145
                    [*Exeunt Attendants.*]
Lucius, all hail, Rome's gracious governor!
                    [*Cries of approval.*]

Lucius. Thanks, gentle Romans: may I govern so,
To heal Rome's harms and wipe away her woe!
But, gentle people, give me aim° awhile,
For nature puts me to a heavy task.   150
Stand all aloof; but, uncle, draw you near
To shed obsequious° tears upon this trunk.
O, take this warm kiss on thy pale cold lips,
These sorrowful drops upon thy bloodstained face,
The last true duties of thy noble son!   155

Marcus. Tear for tear and loving kiss for kiss
Thy brother Marcus tenders on thy lips:

133 *ragged* rugged   134 *mutual closure* common end   149 *give me aim* assist me   152 *obsequious* mourning

O, were the sum of these that I should pay
Countless and infinite, yet would I pay them!

160 *Lucius.* Come hither, boy; come, come, and learn of us
To melt in showers. Thy grandsire loved thee well;
Many a time he danced thee on his knee,
Sung thee asleep, his loving breast thy pillow;
Many a story hath he told to thee,
165 And bid thee bear his pretty tales in mind,
And talk of them when he was dead and gone.

Marcus. How many thousand times hath these poor
lips,
When they were living, warmed themselves on thine!
O, now, sweet boy, give them their latest° kiss.
170 Bid him farewell; commit him to the grave;
Do them° that kindness, and take leave of them.

Boy. O, grandsire, grandsire! Ev'n with all my heart
Would I were dead, so you did live again!
O Lord, I cannot speak to him for weeping;
175 My tears will choke me if I ope my mouth.

[*Enter Attendants with Aaron.*]

Roman. You sad Andronici, have done with woes;
Give sentence on this execrable wretch
That hath been breeder of these dire events.

Lucius. Set him breast-deep in earth and famish him;
180 There let him stand and rave and cry for food:
If anyone relieves or pities him,
For the offense he dies. This is our doom.°
Some stay, to see him fast'ned in the earth.

Aaron. Ah, why should wrath be mute, and fury dumb?
185 I am no baby, I, that with base prayers
I should repent the evils I have done:
Ten thousand worse than ever yet I did
Would I perform, if I might have my will:
If one good deed in all my life I did,

169 *latest* last   171 *them* i.e., "these poor lips" of line 167   182
doom sentence

I do repent it from my very soul.   190

Lucius. Some loving friends convey the Emperor hence,
    And give him burial in his father's grave:
    My father and Lavinia shall forthwith
    Be closèd in our household's monument.
    As for that ravenous tiger, Tamora,   195
    No funeral rite, nor man in mourning weed,
    No mournful bell shall ring her burial;
    But throw her forth to beasts and birds to prey.
    Her life was beastly and devoid of pity,
    And being dead, let birds on her take pity.   *Exeunt.*   200

Finis the Tragedy of Titus Andronicus.

Textual Note

There is an allusion to a Roman hero named Titus in *A Knack to Know a Knave,* acted in June 1592. Though the allusion may, of course, be to an earlier play on the subject rather than to Shakespeare's play, there is no need to multiply entities; Shakespeare's *Titus Andronicus* may have been on the stage before 1592. The next bit of evidence is a reference of 23 January 1594 in Henslowe's *Diary* to the effect that Sussex's men acted a new piece, "titus & ondronicus." If the allusion in *A Knave* is not to Shakespeare's play, quite possibly *Titus Andronicus* was indeed new in 1594, but it is equally possible that it was "new" only to Sussex's company, or that it had been newly revised. On 6 February 1594 the Stationers' Register entered "a book intituled a Noble Roman Historye of Titus Andronicus." Perhaps this entry alludes to the play, which indeed was published in 1594, though possibly the entry is to some other piece on the same subject. In 1614 Ben Jonson, in the Induction to *Bartholomew Fair,* mentions that Andronicus was seen on the stage as long ago as "fiue and twentie or thirtie yeeres"; strictly, Jonson's reference would date the play 1584–89, though probably he is speaking loosely and his evidence surely does not prohibit a date in the early nineties. The date widely favored is 1592–94, but there is no compelling reason to believe that *Titus* could not have been written in the late eighties.

Only one copy of the first quarto (1594) is known to be extant. Apparently Q1 (i.e., the first quarto) was printed from Shakespeare's manuscript or from a copy of it; a number of stage directions—such as "Enter . . . as many as can be"—suggest an author's hand. In 1600 a second quarto (Q2) was issued. It omits a few lines, adds some, and alters a good deal of punctuation. There is no reason to believe that the alterations represent Shakespeare's revisions; probably all the revisions are a compositor's tamperings. Q3, issued in 1611, was set up from Q2 and therefore has no authority. The version in the First Folio (F) is based on Q3 but makes numerous small alterations (especially in stage directions) and adds the entire scene (III.ii). The new scene is of sufficient excellence to be Shakespeare's, and though the other changes in F do not suggest that great effort was made to give the play in a version much different from that of Q3, the new scene shows that the editors had access to some unpublished material. The present edition is based on Q1, except for III.ii, which is, of course, based on F. It regularizes speech prefixes (for example, Q1's "Saturnine," "Saturninus," "King," "Satur," are all given here as "Saturninus"); it slightly alters the position of a few stage directions, and it modernizes spelling and punctuation. The act divisions were first established by F; the scene divisions are the work of later editors and though of no authenticity they provide a convenient device for reference. Departures from Q1, other than those mentioned above and corrections of obvious typographical errors, are listed below, the adopted reading first, in *italic* type, followed by the original reading in roman. If the adopted reading is from Q2, Q3, or F, that fact is indicated in a bracket following the reading. If there is no such indication, the adopted reading is an editor's conjecture.

I.i.35 [for the three and a half lines that follow these words in Q1 see footnote to the line] 69 s.d. *her three sons* her two sonnes 98 *manes* manus 226 *Titan's* [Q2] Tytus 242 *Pantheon* Pathan 264 *chance* [Q2] change 280 *cuique* cuiqum 317 *Phoebe* Thebe 358 s.d. *speak* speakes 369 *Martius* 3. Sonne 370 *Quintus* 2. Sonne 372 *Quintus* 2. sonne 391 [Q1 follows with s.d.:

"Exit all but Marcus and Titus," and the other early texts also indicate an exit]   399 *Yes ... remunerate* [F; omitted in the quartos]

II.i.110 *than* this

II.ii.1 *morn* [F] Moone

II.iii.69 *try* [Q2] trie thy   72 *swart* swartie   160 *ears* [Q3] yeares 210 *unhallowed* [F] vnhollow   222 *berayed* bereaud   231 *Pyramus* [Q2] Priamus   236 *Cocytus* Ocitus

II.iv.27 *him* them   30 *three* their

III.i.146 *his true* her true

III.ii [this scene is found only in F]   39 *complainer* complayne 52 *thy knife* knife   53 *fly* Flys   55 *are cloyed* cloi'd   72 *myself* my selfes

IV.i.50 *quotes* [Q2] coats   88 *hope* [Q2] hop [or "I op"]

IV.ii.95 *Alcides* [Q2] Alciades

IV.iii.57 *Saturn* Saturnine   78 *News* [Q2] Clowne. Newes

IV.iv.5 *know, as know* know   49 *By* be   99 *ears* [F] yeares

V.ii.52 *caves* cares   56 *Hyperion's* Epeons   65 *worldly* [Q2] wordlie

V.iii. 125 *cause* course   144 *adjudged* [F] adiudge   154 *bloodstained* blood slaine   163 *Sung* [Q2] Song

A Note on the Source of
Titus Andronicus

Those Shakespeareans who are embarrassed by *Titus* (but who cannot overlook the strong evidence that he wrote it) sometimes assume that it represents his reworking of an older, and presumably worse, play. No such play has come to light, and though it is possible that Shakespeare's source was a play now extant only in Shakespeare's revision, it is more than possible—even likely—that his source was a prose tale regarded as history. The Folger Shakespeare Library has a unique copy of a mid-eighteenth-century booklet entitled *The History of Titus Andronicus,* which contains a prose narrative (reprinted below) and a ballad. The ballad, of no interest to us, is an abbreviated metrical version of the prose narrative, but this latter seems to be a reprint of a much older piece—quite possibly of a late-sixteenth-century version that may have been Shakespeare's source. Certainly the prose narrative is not indebted to the play: it makes no reference to Shakespeare—as it surely would if it had been written in the eighteenth century—and it includes a good deal of alleged history that Shakespeare does not. Furthermore, some of its characters are unnamed; if the narrative were based on the play, Aaron, for example,

135

would doubtless be mentioned by name, but he is merely called "the wicked Moor."

Put it this way: the extant *History of Titus Andronicus* is almost surely a reprint of a much older piece, quite possibly a reprint of the tale that Shakespeare dramatized. There is no opposing evidence. The *History* is reprinted below, from the only known copy, and for the first time since its publication in the middle of the eighteenth century. Spelling and punctuation have been modernized, and manifest typographical errors have been corrected.

THE
HISTORY
OF
Titus Andronicus,
THE RENOWNED ROMAN GENERAL

who, after he had saved Rome by his valor from being destroyed by the barbarous Goths and lost two and twenty of his valiant sons in ten years' war, was, upon the Emperor's marrying the Queen of the Goths, put to disgrace and banished; but being recalled, the Emperor's son by a first wife was murdered by the Empress' sons and a bloody Moor, and how charging it upon Andronicus' sons, though he cut off his hand to redeem their lives, they were murdered in prison; how his fair daughter Lavinia, being ravished by the Empress' sons, they cut out her tongue, and hands off, etc.; how Andronicus slew them, made pies of their flesh, and presented them to the Emperor and Empress; and then slew them also; with the miserable death he put the wicked Moor to; then at her request slew his daughter and himself to avoid torment.

The
Tragical History
OF
Titus Andronicus, etc.

Chapter I

How Rome being besieged by the barbarous Goths and being at the point to yield through famine, it was unexpectedly rescued by Andronicus, with the utter defeat of the enemy, for which he was received in triumph.

When the Roman Empire was grown to its height and the greatest part of the world was subjected to its imperial throne, in the time of Theodosius, a barbarous northern people out of Swedeland, Denmark, and Gothland came into Italy in such numbers, under the leading of Tottilius, their king, that they overrun it with fire and sword, plundering churches, ripping up women with child, and deflowering virgins in so horrid and barbarous a manner that the people fled before them like flocks of sheep.

To oppose this destroying torrent of the Goths, a barbarous people, strangers to Christianity, the Emperor raised a mighty army in Greece, Italy, France, Spain, Germany, and England, and gave battle under the passage of the Alpine mountains, but was overthrown, with the loss of threescore thousand of his men, and flying to Rome, was besieged in it by a numerous host of these barbarians, who pressed so hard to beat down the walls and enter with a miserable slaughter of the citizens that such as could get over the River Tiber fled in a fearful manner to a distant country. The siege lasting ten months, such a famine arose that no unclean thing was left uneaten; dogs, cats, horses, rats and mice were curious dainties; thousands died in the streets of hunger, and most of those that were alive looked more like glass than living creatures; so that being brought to the last extremity, the vulgar sort came about the Emperor's palace and with piteous cries implored him either to find some means to get them food, to stay their fleeting lives, or make the best terms he could and open the gates to the enemy.

This greatly perplexed him; the former he could not do, and the latter he knew would not only uncrown him, if he escaped with his life, but be the ruin of the Roman Empire; yet in the greatest of this extremity he unexpectedly found relief.

Titus Andronicus, a Roman senator and a true lover of his country, hearing in Graecia, where he was governor of the province of Achaia, what straits Rome and his sovereign were brought into by the barbarous nations, got together friends and sold whatever he had of value to hire soldiers; so that with his small army he secretly marched away, and falling upon the mighty army of the enemy (when they were drowned as it were in security, wine, and sleep, resolved to make a general storm the next day, in which they had undoubtedly carried the city), he and his sons, entering their camp, and followed by the rest, made such a slaughter that the cry and confusion were exceeding great; some changed sleep into death, others vomited wine and blood mixed together, through the wounds they received; some lost heads at once, others arms: Tottilius, in this confusion being awakened, had his first care to convey away his queen and two sons, who were newly come to the camp, and then labored to rally his flying men; but being desperately charged by Andronicus, he was thrown from his horse and much wounded, many lives being lost in remounting him; whereupon seeing the slaughter so great by the pale beams of the moon, and not knowing the number of his adversaries, having caused the retreat to be sounded, he fled in great confusion and left the rich spoils of his camp, the wealth of many plundered nations, to Andronicus and his soldiers; who being expert in war, would not meddle with them that night, but stood to their arms till the morning.

Chapter II

How in ten years' war, with the loss of two and twenty of his valiant sons, he won many famous battles, slew Tottilius, King of the Goths, and did many other brave exploits, etc.

The watch upon the walls of Rome, having heard a confused cry and the clashing of arms, were greatly astonished, but could not think what it should mean; for the camps of the barbarous Goths extended in a large circuit about the famous city; however, the captains of the guards advertised the Emperor of it, who sent out scouts, but they, fearful of approaching too near the enemy in the night, could get certain intelligence only that they heard the groans and cries, as they thought, of dying men. However, the shades of night being dispelled, and the glorious sun raising [?] forth a cheerful light, the porters of the gate espying three men coming towards it, and soon after being come up, knocked with great earnestness, they took the courage to demand what they were and what they required.

"I am," said one of them, "Andronicus, your friend, and desire admittance to speak with the Emperor, since the news I bring will no doubt be pleasing to him."

Upon this, lifting up his helmet, they knew him with joy, knowing him to be a very worthy patriot, thinking he came to do them good, as he had often done in their great distress when the Huns and Vandals invaded the empire some years before and were beaten out by him.

The Emperor no sooner heard he was come, but he ran from his palace to meet him and would not suffer him to kneel, but embraced him tenderly as a brother, saying, "Welcome, Andronicus, in this the time of our greatest misery; it was thy counsel I wanted, to know how to free us from this barbarous enemy, against whose force the city cannot long hold out."

"May it please your Majesty," replied Andronicus, "let

those fears be banished, the work is done to you unknown; I and my twenty-five sons, and what friends and soldiers I could get, have this night fallen into their quarters, cut off fifty thousand of them, and their scattered remains with their king are fled."

At this the Emperor was astonished and scarce could believe it, though he very well knew the integrity of Andronicus, till his own captains came and told him the siege was raised with a miserable slaughter, but by whom they knew not, unless the enemy had fallen out among themselves, and the troops they could yet see in view were but inconsiderable. Now these were those that belonged to Andronicus, who as soon as it was day were in pursuit of the enemy under the command of his five-and-twenty sons.

This surprising news was no sooner spread in the city but the joy of the people was exceeding great; and when they knew who was their deliverer, they went in procession and sung his praises. After that he rode in a triumphant chariot through the city, crowned with an oaken garland, the people shouting, trumpets sounding, and all other expressions and demonstrations of joy that a grateful people could afford their deliverer, in which he behaved himself so humble that he gained the love of all.

This was no sooner over, but he desired the Emperor to join what forces he could with those that he had brought and speedily pursue the enemy before he could gather new strength, that he might beat him out of Italy and his other countries where he yet held strong garrisons. This was embraced as good counsel, and the senators, by the Emperor's mandate, assembled with joy, who chose with one consent Andronicus their general. He was not slow in mustering his forces, nor in the speedy pursuit; he found they had passed the Alps and that their army was increased by new supplies, yet he gave them battle, and charging through the thickest of their squadrons hand to hand, slew Tottilius and beat down his standard. Whereupon the Goths fled, and the slaughter continued for many miles, covering all the lanes and roads with the bodies of the dead; and in the pursuit he took the Queen of the

Goths captive and brought her to Rome, for which signal victory he had a second triumph and was styled the deliverer of his country. But his joy was a little eclipsed by the loss of five of his sons, who died courageously fighting in battle.

Chapter III

How the Emperor, weary of so tedious a war, contrary to the mind and persuasions of Andronicus, married the Queen of the Goths and concluded a peace; how she tyrannized and her sons slew the Prince that was betrothed to Andronicus' daughter and hid him in the forest.

The Goths, having found the pleasantness of these fruitful countries, resolved not so to give them over, but, encouraged by Tottilius' two sons, Alaricus and Abonus, sent for fresh forces and made a desolation in the Roman provinces, continuing a ten years' war, wherein the valiant Andronicus, Captain-General of the Empire, gained many victories over them, with great effusion of blood on either side; but those barbarous people still increasing in their numbers, the Emperor, desiring peace, it was agreed to, in consideration he should marry Attava, Queen of the Goths, and in case he should die without issue, her sons might succeed in the Empire. Andronicus opposed this very much, as did many other, knowing, through the Emperor's weakness, that she, being an imperious woman and of a haughty spirit, would govern him as she pleased and enslave the noble Empire to strangers. However, it was carried on with a high hand, and great preparations were made for the royal nuptials, though with very little rejoicing among the people, for what they expected soon followed.

The Queen of the Goths being made Empress, soon began to show her disposition, according to the cruelty of her nation and temper, persuading the easy Emperor to place the Goths in the places of his most trusty friends;

and having above all vowed revenge on Andronicus, who most opposed her proceedings, she procured him to be banished; but the people, whose deliverer he had been in their greatest extremity, calling to mind that and his many other good services, rose unanimously in arms and went clamoring to the palace, threatening to fire it and revenge so base an indignity on the Queen, if the decree which had been passed against all reason was not speedily revoked. This put her and the Emperor into such a fears [sic] that their request was granted; and now she plotted by more private ways to bring the effects of revenge and implacable hatred about more secretly.

She had a Moor as revengeful as herself, whom she trusted in many great affairs and was usually privy to her secrets, so far that from private dalliances she grew pregnant and brought forth a blackamoor child. This grieved the Emperor extremely, but she allayed his anger by telling him it was conceived by the force of imagination, and brought many suborned women and physicians to testify the like had often happened. This made the Emperor send the Moor into banishment, upon pain of death never to return to Rome. But her lust and the confidence she had put in him as the main engine to bring about her devilish designs made her plot to have that decree revoked; when having got the Emperor into a pleasant humor, she feigned herself sick, telling him withal she had seen a vision which commanded her to call back the innocent Moor from banishment or she should never recover of that sickness. The kind, good-natured Emperor, who could not resist her tears and entreaties, with some difficulty consented to it, provided he should be commanded to keep always out of her sight, lest the like mischance might happen as had been before. This she seemingly consented to, and he was immediately sent for, and the former familiarities continued between them, though more privately.

Andronicus, besides his sons, had a very fair and beautiful daughter, named Lavinia, brought up in all singular virtues, humble, courteous, and modest, insomuch that the Emperor's only son, by a former wife, fell extremely in love with her, seeking her favor by all virtuous and honorable ways, insomuch that after a long courtship, with her father and the Emperor's consent she was betrothed to him.

The Queen of the Goths, hearing this, was much enraged, because from such a marriage might spring princes that might frustrate her ambitious designs, which was to make her sons emperors jointly. Wherefore she labored all she could to frustrate it, by declaring what a disgrace it would be to the Emperor to marry his son to the daughter of a subject, who might have a queen with a kingdom to her dowry. But finding the Prince constant, she resolved to take him out of the way; so it was plotted between her, the Moor, and her two sons that they should invite him to hunt in the great forest on the banks of the River Tiber, and there murder him. This was effected, by shooting him through the back with a poisoned arrow, which came out at his breast, of which wound he fell from his horse and immediately died. Then they digged a very deep pit in a pathway and threw him in, covering it lightly with boughs and sprinkling earth on it; and so returning reported they had lost the Prince in the forest, and though they had sought and called everywhere, they could not find him.

Chapter IV

How the wicked Moor, who had laid with the Empress and got into her favor above all others, betrayed Andronicus' three sons and charged the Prince's murder on them, for which they were cast into a dungeon, and after their father had cut off his hand to save them were beheaded.

The fair Lavinia no sooner heard the Prince was missing but she fell into great sorrow and lamentation, her heart misgiving her of some treachery, and thereupon she entreated her brothers to go in search of him, which they did with all speed. But being dogged by the Moor and the Queen of Goths's two sons, they unluckily coming in the way where the pit was digged, they fell both in upon the dead body and could not by reason of the great depth get out. Their cruel enemies no sooner saw this, but they hasted to the court and sent the guards in search of the murdered Prince, who found Andronicus' two sons with the dead body, which they drew up and carried prisoners to the court, where the Moor and the other two falsely swore against them that they had often heard them threaten revenge on the Prince, because he had put them to the foil, in a tournament at jousting. This, and the circumstances of their being found, with the vehement aggravation, was a sufficient ground to the Emperor to believe, who loved his son entirely and was much grieved for his death, and though they denied it with all the protestations imaginable, and pleaded their innocence, demanded the combat against their accusers, which by the law of arms they ought to have been allowed, they were immediately loaden with irons and cast into a deep dungeon among noisome creatures, as frogs, toads, serpents, and the like, where notwithstanding all the intercessions that were made they continued eating the filth that they found in that place.

At last the Queen, designing to work her revenge on Andronicus, sent the Moor in the Emperor's name, to tell him, if he designed to save his sons from the misery and death that would ensue, he should cut off his right hand and send it to court. This the good-natured father scrupled not to do, no, nor had it been his life to ransom them, he would have freely parted with it; whereupon laying his hand on a block, he gave the wicked Moor his sword, who immediately struck it off and inwardly laughed at the villainy. Then departing with it, he told him his sons should be sent to him in a few hours. But whilst he was rejoicing with the hopes of their delivery, a hearse came to his door with guards, which made his aged heart to tremble. The first thing they presented him was his hand, which they said would not be accepted; and the next was his three sons beheaded. At this woeful sight, overcome with grief, he fainted away on the dead bodies; and when he recovered again, he tore his hoary hair, which age and

his lying in winter camps for the defense of his country
had made as white as snow, pouring out floods of tears;
but found no pity from the hardened villains, who left
him with scoffs in the midst of his woeful lamentations
with his sorrowful daughter. Yet this was not all, for soon
after another to be deplored affliction followed, as shall
in the next chapter be shown.

Chapter V

*How the two lustful sons of the Empress, with the as-
sistance of the Moor, in a barbarous manner ravished
Lavinia, Andronicus' beautiful daughter, and cut out her
tongue and cut off her hands, to prevent discovery; yet
she did it by writing in the dust with a wand, etc.*

The fair and beautiful Lavinia, for the loss of her lovers [*sic*] and brothers, so basely murdered by treachery,
tore her golden hair, shed floods of tears, and with her
nails offered violence to that lovely face kings had adored
and beheld with admiration. She shunned all company,
retiring to woods and groves, to utter her piteous com-
plaints and cries to the senseless trees, when one day, being watched thither by the Moor, he gave notice of it to
the Queen's two sons, who, like the wicked Elders and
chaste Susanna, had a long time burned in lust yet knew
her virtues were proof against all temptations, and therefore it could not be obtained but by violence. So thinking this an opportunity to serve their turns, immediately
repaired to the grove and setting the Moor to watch on
the outborders, soon found her pensive and sorrowful, yet
comely and beautiful in tears, when unawares, before she
saw them, like two ravenous tigers, they seized the trem-
bling lady, who struggled all she could and cried out piteously for help; and seeing what their wicked intentions
bent at, she offered them her throat, desiring they would
bereave her of her life, but not of her honor. However, in
a villainous manner, staking her down by the hair of her

head and binding her hands behind her, they turned up
her nakedness and forced their way into her closet of
chastity, taking it by turns, the elder beginning first and
the younger seconding him as they had before agreed
on; and having tired themselves in satiating their beastly
appetites, they began to consider how they should come
off when such a villainy was discovered. Whereupon, calling the Moor to them, they asked his advice, who wickedly
counseled them to make all sure, seeing they had gone
thus far, by cutting out her tongue to hinder her telling
tales and her hands off to prevent her writing a discovery.
This the cruel wretches did, whilst she in vain entreated
them to take away her life, since they had bereaved her
of her honor, which was dearer to her. And in this woeful
condition they left the lady, who had expired for the loss
of blood had not her uncle Marcus happened accidentally,
soon after, to come in search of her, who at the woeful
sight, overcome with sorrow, could hardly keep life in
himself; yet recovering his spirits, he bound up her
wounds and conveyed her home.

Poor Andronicus' grief for this sad disaster was so
great that no pen can write or words express; much ado
they had to restrain him from doing violence upon himself; he cursed the day he was born to see such miseries
fall on himself and family, entreating her to tell him, if
she could any ways do it by signs, who had so villainously
abused her. At last the poor lady, with a flood of tears
gushing from her eyes, taking a wand between her stumps,
wrote these lines:

> The lustful sons of the proud Empress
> Are doers of this hateful wickedness.

Hereupon he vowed revenge, at the hazard of his own
and all their lives, comforting his daughter with this when
nothing else would do.

Chapter VI

*How Andronicus, feigning himself mad, found means to
entrap the Empress' two sons in a forest, where, binding
them to a tree, he cut their throats, made pies of their
flesh, and served them up to the Emperor and Empress,
then slew them, set the Moor quick in the ground, and
then killed his daughter and himself.*

Andronicus, upon these calamities, feigned himself dis-
tracted and went raving about the city, shooting his
arrows towards heaven, as in defiance, calling to hell for
vengeance, which mainly pleased the Empress and her
sons, who thought themselves now secure; and though his
friends required justice of the Emperor against the ravishers, yet they could have no redress, he rather threatening
them, if they insisted on it; so that finding they were in
a bad case and that in all probability their lives would
be the next, they conspired together to prevent that mischief and revenge themselves; lying in ambush in the
forest when the two sons went a-hunting, they surprised
them, and binding them to a tree pitifully crying out for
mercy, though they would give none to others, Andronicus
cut their throats whilst Lavinia, by his command, held a
bowl between her stumps to receive the blood; then con-
veying the bodies home to his own house privately, he cut
the flesh into fit pieces and ground the bones to powder
and made of them two mighty pasties, and invited the
Emperor and Empress to dinner, who, thinking to make
sport with his frantic humor, came; but when they had
eat of the pasties, he told them what it was; and thereupon giving the watchword to his friends, they immediately issued out, slew the Emperor's guards, and, lastly,
the Emperor and his cruel wife, after they had sufficiently
upbraided them with the wicked deeds they had done.
Then seizing on the wicked Moor, the fearful villain fell
on his knees, promising to discover all. But when he had
told how he had killed the Prince, betrayed the three sons

of Andronicus by false accusation, and counseled the abuse to the fair Lavinia, they scarce knew what torments sufficient to devise for him; but at last digging a hole, they set him in the ground to the middle alive, smeared him over with honey, and so, between the stinging of bees and wasps and starving, he miserably ended his wretched days. After this, to prevent the torments he expected when these things came to be known, at his daughter's request he killed her; and so, rejoicing he had revenged himself on his enemies to the full, fell on his own sword and died.

Commentaries

H. T. PRICE

from *The Authorship of "Titus Andronicus"*

The best "parallel" by which we can test authorship is
construction. Phrases may be borrowed here and there,
but construction refers to the planning of the work as a
whole. It is the most intimate expression of the author's
meaning. Lyly, indeed, taught Shakespeare certain details
of balance. But the pupil soon outstripped his teacher, and
the masterly use Shakespeare made of what he learned
gives him a place apart among Elizabethan dramatists.
The carriage of the plot and the weaving together of many
motifs to form unity require a particular kind of skill without which all outside aid is futile.

The closest parallel to *Titus* is the plot of *Lear*. Here
as there we have two parties, whom we may crudely call
the good and the bad. In both there are different kinds of
good men opposed to different kinds of bad. Some critics

From *The Journal of English and Germanic Philology*, XLII (1943).
Reprinted by permission of the author and the publisher.

find that the plot of *Titus* is weakened because the leadership of the "bad" party varies. It is now in the hands of Tamora, now with Aaron. I do not think this criticism has any force, since this variation does nothing to impede the sweep and rush of the play. In any case there is the same thing in *Lear*. Sometimes it is Goneril, sometimes it is Edmund, who takes the lead against Lear. In both plays the effect is the same. The forces of evil, no matter who embodies them, work with unabated intensity until the climax is reached.

If then one is looking for parallels, the only parallel to the plot of *Titus* is to be found in the other works of Shakespeare. Greene and Peele are so loose and episodic, so naïve in construction that it is incredible that they should have achieved anything so good as *Titus*. Nor is there any plot of Marlowe's so intricate, so varied, or so well sustained. *Titus* is the expression of a conflict intenser than anything the Elizabethan stage had as yet known. Shakespeare applies in *Titus* those principles of balance and contrast which he had learned from Lyly and had already tested in comedy. He sets up against one another two parties, each led by formidable characters. It is the play of fence between the high incensed points of these mighty opposites that makes the drama. There is nothing like this in Marlowe, whose supermen dominate his plays and dwarf everybody else in them. There is nothing like it in Greene and Peele, who indeed lacked the personality to create a drama of tense conflict.

Titus then resembles Shakespeare's other work, both comedy and tragedy, in that it is built upon the principle of contrast. We have the contrasting pairs or groups: Titus-Aaron, Lavinia-Tamora, Saturninus-Bassianus, the sons of Titus—the sons of Tamora. Not only are members of the opposite party contrasted, there are also contrasts within the same party. Marcus, as we shall see, by his mildness throws into higher relief the sterner traits of Titus. Contrast dominates the play and informs every scene of it. As we have already noted, whatever is fine in the Romans appears finer still in comparison with the vices of their opposites. On the one hand we have courage, stern probity, honor, but also stubbornness, hardness, and stupidity; on the other hand, slipperiness, trickiness, intrigue, the lie, foulness of every sort. None of the dramatists who are supposed to have had a hand in the play could conceive a plan so intricate or adhere to it so closely, once it was conceived. But Shakespeare goes farther. He uses contrast to heighten incident and situation as well as character. Act II.ii and iii are admirable examples of Shakespeare's technique. The delightful freshness of dawn and the beauty of the woods are not described for their own sake, still less are they, as some critics assert, a homesick reminiscence of Stratford. They are written in cold blood with the deliberate purpose of accentuating by contrast the horrors that follow. Shakespeare is again borrowing from the technique of Seneca.

There are few things in the play so characteristic of Shakespeare as the function of Marcus. In a world of hard, fierce, revengeful men, he alone is given to gentleness and moderation. Shakespeare often employs this device of a character who embodies a principle standing in stark contrast to the motives that rule the other persons of the play. We have, for instance, Falstaff in *1 Henry IV*. Marcus resembles most closely Henry VI in *2, 3 Henry VI,* the mild, kind king, averse from slaughter and, like Marcus, helpless among so many Kiplingesque heroes. Frequently scholars declare that characters thus marked off are the "mouthpiece" of Shakespeare. However that may be, the technique is just what we should expect to find in a play by Shakespeare. We do not expect to find it in Marlowe, Greene, or Peele.

There is a school of critics who apply the "law of variation" to this technique. They ignore the part that contrast plays in Shakespeare's genuine work and they fasten upon the contrasting elements in *Titus* as evidence of multiple authorship. They usually say that the "poetic" passages, especially the speeches of Marcus, cannot be by the same hand as the rest of the play. Or they declare that the rhetorical speeches of Act I are so different from the imaginative verse of Aaron that there must be two poets at work. Anybody who is inclined to follow their lead should study Titania-Bottom, The Nurse-Juliet, Hotspur-Falstaff, Iago-Othello, and then, if he dares, set limits to the unparalleled versatility of Shakespeare.

Act I is often condemned as being utterly un-Shakespearean. Anglo-Saxon critics are inclined to apply a verbal yardstick to drama and to ignore construction. The act is not finely enough phrased for such people and so they reject it. Technically it is one of the finest first acts that Shakespeare wrote. It is full of incident and yet it is never confused. It announces the subject boldly and unmistakably, it exploits to the full every device that the staging of those days offered, and it has swiftness, surprise, and a well-sustained interest. It leads up to an effective close. Nothing in the work of Shakespeare's contemporaries can be compared to it for a moment.

The plot is superior to anything that Greene, Peele, Marlowe, or Kyd could achieve, by its quick succession of closely knit incidents, enlivened by many sudden turns and surprises, by its intricacy, in that the fates of so many persons are involved in it and yet the thread is never lost, and by the skill with which all the different threads are bound up into one knot and untied at once in the fifth act. Intricacy with clearness, a firm hand on the story, a swift succession of effective situations logically leading out of what precedes and on to what follows, these are qualities lacking in the dramatists who are supposed to have shared in the composition of *Titus*.

It must be admitted that the plot hinges on several Elizabethan conventions that are now strange to us. For instance the ruse, no matter how transparent, always succeeds, first when Titus is tricked, later when Titus himself takes to deception. Aaron eavesdrops in II.i—the Elizabethans took in this trick a childish delight which we cannot recapture. Quite suddenly Saturninus falls head over heels in love with Tamora—the Elizabethan believed in these swift and overwhelming effects of passion. Shakespeare is full of them. (See Ruth L. Anderson, *Elizabethan Psychology and Shakespeare's Plays,* Iowa, 1928, p. 120.) Every dramatist must work according to the rules of the game as it is understood in his time. The play is not less likely to be by Shakespeare because it is so full of the conventions of the theater.

We come to an important aspect of the plot which scholars tend to overlook. *Titus* is a political play, and Shakespeare is the most political of all dramatists. His work excited the admiration of statesmen like Gladstone and Bismarck, who both wondered how he managed to penetrate so many secrets of their profession. Shakespeare's political interest shows itself in various ways. He likes to connect his heroes with an action involving the fortunes of the state, he is skillful in tracing the course of political intrigue, and he delights in exposing those kinks of character or intellect which unfit even men of action for public life. The real hero of his political plays is the state. In some plays it is England, in others it is Rome. Now *Titus* centers round an affair of state, and its hero is no particular person but it is Rome herself. All the characters are viewed in their relation to Rome and they are set against Rome as a background. This theme is sustained throughout the play; it dominates the fifth act as the first. No member of that writers' syndicate—large as it is—which the revisionists credit with *Titus* has Shakespeare's deep love of the state or his understanding of the crisscross currents of politics. The intense political interest of *Titus* points to the man who wrote Shakespeare's historical and Roman plays, and it points to no one else.

But even if we grant that *Titus* could not have been written by anybody but Shakespeare, its horrible cruelty still leaves us profoundly dissatisfied. It is not only that Titus is cruel; it is more, he is cruel to the end. He is not a Lear who grows in stature as the play proceeds and whose sufferings purge his character of its baser elements until he emerges a man entirely good. Titus alone of Shakespeare's tragic heroes never arrives at healing self-knowledge. At the beginning of the play we hope that Titus will succeed against his enemies; at the end we wish that he had not. But we must not forget the task that Shakespeare has set himself. He is writing a Senecan play according to the rules, that is to say, a play in which the hero is a man who inexorably pursues revenge and who

dies in the act of taking it. Such a plan leaves no room
for change of character. Shakespeare, therefore, has been
obliged to split what he had to say between Titus and
Marcus. Roughly speaking, Lear is a Titus who becomes
a Marcus, but a revenge play necessarily precluded this
type of development. Shakespeare has not been deluded
into thinking revenge is a fine thing. He sets up Marcus
to show us the better way. The great fault of the drama
from our point of view is that Titus never finds that way.
But his stern pursuit of revenge is inherent in the revenge
play and Shakespeare could only have got round it by
making his hero a kind of Hamlet.

Now if we could absolve Shakespeare of all complicity
in the revenge play of *Titus Andronicus,* that might be a
good thing. Unfortunately, the evidence makes it quite
clear that Shakespeare is at any rate an accessory to the
crime, and that he is responsible for the play as it now
stands. It is more profitable to consider what probably
took place. Everyone knows the cant phrase that Shakespeare "played the sedulous ape" to all and sundry. Even
late in life he is asserted to have copied Beaumont and
Fletcher. In his apprentice stage he founded himself on
Lyly, on Marlowe, and went to Roman comedy, to
Plautus. In the same way, in order to learn his craft, he
went to Roman tragedy, to Seneca. To understand this,
we must remember that the Renaissance entertained an
immense admiration for Seneca and that it was the fashion
to imitate him. Shakespeare, following the mood of his
time, wrote a complete Senecan tragedy, an experiment of
unity in harshness and gross cruelty. He makes almost
everything harsh, the language, the characters, the incidents. Where he appears to be relenting toward mildness,
that is only an artistic device to make the harshness appear all the harsher. It is the very unity of the play that
is a criterion of Shakespeare's skill. It is, indeed, this
severe unity, which is difficult to achieve, that makes it
impossible to entertain the theory that this play was the
work of a syndicate of writers or of some young amateur
helped out by Shakespeare.

If we turn from the action to the character shown in

action, we are just as certainly within the realm of Shakespeare. There is no convincing parallel to the character of Titus outside the works of Shakespeare. He owes, indeed, a few hints to Kyd's *Spanish Tragedy*. Like Kyd's Hieronimo he is an old man angry, seeking revenge for murder, but in the essentials of characterization he is quite different. Titus, like the typical Shakespearean hero, falls by a mixture of good and bad qualities. He is a soldier, and as such, put loyalty and obedience before everything. In his campaigns he has been accustomed both to judge men swiftly and to act swiftly on his judgment. But he has something of the simplicity of Othello; although he can estimate a man's capacity in the field, he is helpless in the hands of a dishonest schemer at home. Like Lear he is a man grown irascible with age, tolerating no insubordination from his inferiors, from whom he demands that unquestioning obedience which he in turn gives to lawful authority. Shakespeare knew that there is nothing so cruel as the wrath of age. Titus is an old man who retains the strength but has lost the elasticity of youth. His fury, therefore, persists with an obstinacy that it is useless to oppose. The murders that Titus commits in Act I are horrible, just as it is horrible of Lear to banish from his heart Cordelia and Kent, but in neither case is the characterization improbable. Critics are inclined to find both Titus and Lear absurd, but Shakespeare knew more about old age than his critics.

As with many soldiers, the religion of Titus is a firm and somewhat naïve acceptance of the usages consecrated by tradition. He kills Alarbus not so much out of cruelty, but because the traditional rites of religion demand it. He makes Saturninus Emperor for much the same reason. Sacred tradition requires that the eldest son of the Emperor should succeed. He stabs his son Mutius in wrath but also as a soldier exacting that same obedience which is the rule of his own life. Some German scholars doubt whether Shakespeare meant us to approve when Titus kills his son! (Wolfgang Keller in *Shaks. Jbch.,* LXXIV [1938], 146). Surely in all the blunders of Titus we see the corruption of the best turned to the worst, qualities

fine in themselves producing disaster because of Titus'
devotion to a false ideal. Further, Titus' habit of loyalty
keeps him blind to the dangers that threaten him. His own
probity makes it difficult for him to suspect duplicity in
others. When the Emperor proves false, his world breaks
down and he begins to go mad. The kaleidoscope is shifted
to show now one side of his character, and now another.
He is not like Marlowe's heroes, the incarnation of a
single quality or passion. He is a mixture of virtues and
weaknesses, and by a strange irony his virtues are the
more devastating. Tamora expresses the fatal defect in his
character when she speaks of "cruel irreligious piety."
A similar ironic treatment is found in other tragedies of
Shakespeare—but nowhere in the work of dramatists who
are supposed to have shared in *Titus*. It was indeed far
beyond their reach. This irony permeates the play so thor-
oughly that scholars would find it difficult to prove that
any part of *Titus* is not by Shakespeare.

Aaron's character, too, is turned round from side to
side so that we can view him from many angles. He is
the obvious villain, black like the devil, lustful, cunning,
cruel, a consummate dissembler and hypocrite, admiring
himself for his superiority in evil and taking a childlike
pleasure in contemplating his villainies. Before the days
of the dictators, the picture was probably thought to be
crude and overdrawn. Shakespeare goes on to mark off
Aaron vividly by allowing him an "Oriental" imagination. He is the only man in the play to speak lines afire
with romantic poetry (see the opening speech of Act II),
as he is the only character to delight in magnificent dress
(II.i.18–20). In this he supplies the strongest possible
contrast with the sober Romans, but he is very like the
Moorish Prince of Arragon in the *Merchant of Venice*
—another parallel that connects Shakespeare with *Titus*.
Suddenly at the end of the play another twist is given to
Aaron's character. He is a devoted father, through the
fact of fatherhood exalted by pride of race and contempt
for the white men, ready to go to any lengths to save his
offspring. Shakespeare does not make the mistake of soft-
ening Aaron to sentimentality by the sight of his child.

He remains a killer. Several of these qualities are found in some Moor or other in the Elizabethan drama, but not all together in the same person. It is his many-sidedness that makes Aaron unique. And even when we add up these characteristics we do not obtain the sum of Aaron. There is a fire, a vigor, and a concentration in his personality such as no Elizabethan villain in the early nineties had displayed. The dilemma is not that either Shakespeare or a rival poet created Aaron, it is *aut Shakespeare, aut diabolus*.

Of the minor figures I will only take young Lucius, since he closely resembles Shakespeare's other boys. His character is composed of that mingled web in which Shakespeare delights. He is on the border between child and man. He weeps at the sight of his grandfather's distress. When Lavinia wants one of his books, he runs away from the girl in fear—a touch that while adding horror to horror shows delicate perception of a child's soul. He is full of big words about the great things he is going to do when he grows up. On the other hand he delivers with courage and address the dangerous message entrusted to him, showing an impish humor that we find in other boys of Shakespeare. His speeches are suited to his age by a somewhat simple vocabulary and a certain lilt in their rhythm. This again is characteristic of Shakespeare's presentation of young boys and girls. There is so much delicacy of perception, sympathy, and humor in the portrait of Lucius that he may take rank with the best of Shakespeare's boys.

Scholars, of course, might recognize Shakespeare's hand in particular characters and still assert that he did no more than just revise the play. But if we look at the characterization broadly, we must say of it what we said of the construction, that it is beyond the reach of anybody but Shakespeare. It is in the round. On the other hand Marlowe's "figures are as one dimensional as a line," and the same is true of Greene and Peele. Besides, the characterization has the peculiar exuberance, the irrepressible vitality which we find in Shakespeare's early work and nowhere else. No other playwright of that pe-

riod could carry such a crowd of persons in his brain
and make them so different from one another and so
alive. More important than this—no other dramatist writing in 1594 could conceive or depict so intense a conflict
of character. Tamora, Aaron, and Titus are as full of
fight as an egg is of meat. Marlowe may fill one man
with consuming passion, Kyd may spin a long intrigue,
but only Shakespeare could combine these things, give
intense passions to a crowd of characters, manipulate
the action and reaction of feeling back and forth from
one character to another, and at the same time keep up
a long intrigue white hot with sustained fury. The sheer,
unflagging power of *Titus* is beyond the reach of anybody but Shakespeare.

Style now remains to be considered as a criterion.
There are two ways of approaching the question—the
philological and the aesthetic. The philologist counts and
compares—his results we have already discussed. It is
only necessary to say here that if parallels prove anything, it is that Shakespeare wrote *Titus*. Aesthetic consideration is more difficult. You cannot say of Shakespeare,
as you can of Ben Jonson and Milton, that he had one
particular style. He was the dramatist speaking through
the minds of his characters, and the words are those of
his characters, not his own. The variations of Shakespeare's style from play to play or from character to character within the same play are among the commonplaces
of criticism.

The question is complicated because Shakespeare was
a slow learner, who made his way by imitating his contemporaries. His early work therefore contains many passages written in the prevailing fashion which just for that
reason offend our taste. Even the great parting scene at
dawn in *Romeo and Juliet* is spoiled for us by lines which
we find too "conceited" or too fantastic. Indeed, ideas
of decorum have changed so much that I doubt if we
can read a single play of Shakespeare's without constantly
being pulled up by passages that are hard for us to accept.

Let us see what the author of *Titus* was doing. He
was writing, as it were, an artificial play, that is one in

a particular mode, according to strict, conventional rules. He is writing the rhetorical drama of Seneca. Professor W. F. Schirmer has worked out for us the rhetorical pattern of this play (*Shaks. Jbch.,* LXXI [1935], pp. 11–31). Professor Schirmer shows that Marcus's speech (I.i.18–45) is exactly divided out into three parts. Two of 7 lines each, consisting of a single sentence, frame a middle part of 14 lines. Part 1 reproaches the Romans for their factional spirit and recommends Titus. Part 2 emphasizes his great merits, his noble character, his achievements, the death in battle of his sons. Part 3 seeks to calm down the rivals. Schirmer points out how this exact logical construction corresponds to the best rules of Quintilian or Cicero (p. 19). There is no room here to follow Schirmer further. It is enough to say that he has shown that a large part of the play is severely rhetorical and that in this respect it resembles much of Shakespeare's early work. Indeed, Shakespeare never completely succeeded in freeing himself from the influence of rhetoric. It not only colors his poetry but it also inspires some of his greatest prose speeches. We all recognize that the sheer beauty of Falstaff's style is the result of a training in rhetoric. Intricately designed speech such as we have in *Titus* is common throughout Shakespeare. If we are looking for affinities, I suggest one that is too often neglected—*Titus,* like *Julius Caesar* and *Coriolanus,* is a political play, in which the hero is Rome, and in which a crisis is time and again resolved by rhetoric. The author of all three plays was a fine historian and a fine rhetorician. I submit that it would be difficult to find an affinity more convincing.

But the style, though rhetorical, is not therefore entirely undramatic. The Romans, the Goths, Aaron, all speak a different language. At this period Shakespeare conceived the Romans as a forthright people, direct in expression, cultivating simplicity in language as in all things. On great occasions their speech can be noble, pity or indignation can move them to poetry, but they are not in the habit of indulging in highfalutin stuff which would lead to a succession of poetical speeches. It is true that in trying to be plain Shakespeare is occasionally flat. But on the whole we can say that the language of the Romans is neat in its plainness and at times it even achieves a kind of monumental dignity. In all his Roman plays Shakespeare aims at some kind of simplicity for his Romans. It is not the same in each play, but then his art ripens.

As we have already noticed, Aaron the Moor speaks with more imagination than anybody else in the play. His ordinary language, however, is full of blunt and coarse expressions that are never to be found in the Roman speeches. Chiron and Demetrius are even coarser than Aaron. They are marked off by their extensive use of rustic proverbs. The Romans do not use proverbs in this way. Tamora, as Professor Schirmer has shown, is all deceit and she can sing any tune. She speaks the language of the man she is talking to. Such differentiation is not to be found in Shakespeare's rivals of the nineties. Other playwrights had their own style, which they gave, together with a characteristic rhythm, to all their persons alike. Shakespeare, on the other hand, takes great pains to differentiate, so that when in the 1590's we find characters carefully distinguished by their style, we may with confidence look upon that as a sign of Shakespeare's authorship. This assertion is so painfully obvious that it would not be worth saying if scholars had not applied the law of variation to the style of *Titus* and attempted to make it prove multiple authorship.

H. B. CHARLTON

from *Shakespearian Tragedy*

Titus Andronicus is melodrama, the crudest of Shakespeare's tragedies, magnificent only in this, that its language is always adequate to its own dramatic and theatrical demands, crude or low, spectacular or sentimental, as on varying occasion they may be. But as drama it can never disguise its own quality. It is a rudimentary type of tragedy. It appeals only to the eye and to the other senses. Response to it is confined to the nervous system. Its thrills and throbs are not transmissible to the mind in forms more intellectual than mere sensation. They induce a nightmare of horrors. As sensations of horror, if they are felt as such at all and not laughed off by man's sense of the ludicrous, they strike so heavily and so frequently that the mind is incapacitated from attempting to translate them into its own discursive idiom. So great is the weight of horror that the response of the senses themselves is finally stunned to stupor, and the disabled sensibility is deprived of the power to prompt mind and imagination to cope with such tremendous issues as are the essence of tragedy, the ultimate mysteries of human

From *Shakespearian Tragedy* by H. B. Charlton. London and New York: Cambridge University Press, 1948. Reprinted by permission of Cambridge University Press.

destiny. "Those who employ spectacular means to create a sense not of the terrible, but only of the monstrous, are strangers to the purpose of Tragedy."[1]

As a piece of serious drama, *Titus Andronicus* has little of worth except its theatrically stirring situations. Even these occur in isolation. A momentary spectacle can be given as much conviction as is needed for the achievement of its stage effect by craftsmanship of no higher order in the art of poetry than is the stage carpenter's in the art of drama. But a sustained representation of human action in a continuous dramatic plot makes greater demands. As Aristotle put it, what happens must happen according to the law of the probable and the necessary. As human action, it must be intelligible. The men and women in the play must act as human beings do act. When their action seems to be spontaneously prompted by passion or by instinct rather than by considered choice, those passions and instincts must be shown to be of that sort which in our experience of life seems likely to break out in that way. When the doers of such deeds plead also the sanction of deliberate choice, the systems of conduct to which they appeal must appear to have impetus vital enough to make their compulsion inevitable. However, a qualification must here be made. Sanctions, like the systems of law and morality which give them their warrant, are but rarely eternal and are often flagrantly ephemeral. *Omnia mutantur, nos et mutamur in illis. Autres temps, autres mœurs.* But in drama, sanctions which are pleaded as constraints to a decisive course of action must have something more than a merely historic warrant to give them effective dramatic force. The compulsion must be felt by the audience as a power which might well compel human beings to such deeds.

It is in respects such as this that the greatest French classical drama seems to an Englishman less universal and therefore less tragic than Shakespeare's tragedies. Their preference for pitting love against honor in the tragic conflict appears, to a modern, to commit them to a contest between unequally matched opponents. The dic-

[1] Aristotle, *Poetics*, XIV, 2 (Butcher).

tates of love may vary from era to era; its nature may swing through a whole range between lust and the lyric love which is half-angel: but love is a passion, an affection deeply rooted even in the physiological genes of spiritual man. There is no limit to its potential urgency as an impulse to action. On the other hand, honor is a code of human construction, and the course of its formulation can be easily watched through a relatively short stretch of historic time. Its taboos and its injunctions are the patent outcome of particular forms of society at particular periods of history. Hence its content embraces manners as much as, and often more than, morals. Its edicts tend therefore to seem arbitrary and even factitious; and as imperatives they have but temporary and local authority. They lack the absoluteness of a universal tragic sanction. Sometimes one of the opposing stresses is formulated in a phrase which seems a limitedly localized or a dialectal idiom; but often this is only the accident of phrase or of manner, and the real significance is clear. Antigone must bury her exiled brother; but the burial itself is only the ritual action symbolizing the real compunction by which the act itself is categorically imperative, the absolute obligation of fraternal duty. Contrast Racine; though the surge of his Phèdre's love can sweep us into conviction of its fury, and, on the other hand, the obligation on her to suppress it or to die can be felt as the command of a code of honor with foundations firmly based in the depths of morality, yet the momentousness of such contending and mighty opposites suffers a sharp collapse on our discovery that the honor of Phèdre, whilst permitting her maid to make wicked charges against Hippolyte, can recover itself by laying all the blame onto this poor servant whose only motive was devotion to her mistress. Often, to drive his action forward with the sense of irresistible compulsion, the dramatist will invoke an impetus from sources outside the will, blind or deliberate, of his persons. At worst, he may allege any extraneous and intrusive determinant as a mere chance, relying on his audience superstitiously to identify chance within some pattern or other of purposive destiny. No great tragedian, however, fails to introduce amongst the operant powers which direct the stream of his plot those cosmic forces which lie beyond human personality and outside the established formularies of human cognition. In the dramatist's summoning of these great mysteries as actors in his drama, his tragic genius is revealed in its deepest qualities. His greatness as a tragedian depends on the extent to which he can invest these superhuman arbiters with the absoluteness of ultimate Necessity. In Shakespeare, this dramatic ultimacy inheres in and also exists outside his characters. For him the stern necessity of character and the resistless compulsion of circumstance are a form of what John Morley called "the modern and positive expression for the old Destiny of the Greeks."

With a mind conscious of these considerations, turn to *Titus Andronicus* and inquire how far its action is autonomously and organically propelled. Very soon, its nominal hero, Titus, is a comparative pawn in the theatrical game, and the real protagonists are the villains, Aaron and Tamora. The incidents of the play, and especially the more theatrical of them, proceed in the main as the deliberate purposes of the villains' evil designs. These purposes are those of sinners whose prevalent passion is lust, than which no passion is more deeply seated in the human animal, none more primary or more insatiable. The dramatist can therefore permit to them the extremest of enormities; the law of human probability can be pleaded for suspending for them its own normal requirements; as Aristotle says, "such an event is probable in Agathon's sense of the word: 'it is probable,' he says, 'that many things should happen contrary to probability.' "[2] Moreover, with such human devils as these for the outstanding figures, other characters and episodes in the play can be stretched to extravagant limits. Titus in his turn can execute his own son. In these ways, the dramatist is easily provided with a string of melodramatic incidents in unbroken sequence. But it is merely the sequence of succession, each item owing its occurrence not

2 *Poetics*, XVIII, 6 (Butcher).

to what has gone immediately before, but as the accidental next in the cumulative outcome of the bestial passions of the main contrivers.

There is, however, some attempt to give to this succession a specious appearance of causal sequence. Action is sometimes expressed, not as the spontaneous consequence of passion, but as the recognizable manifestation of some sort of world order.

The first scene sets up the façade of the universe in which its action is to occur. The "righteous heavens," "the gods of Rome" preside over it; priests minister at their solemn services, sometimes with "holy water," sometimes with "sacrificial rites"; its men lift up their "vows to heaven," and "sumptuously" maintain the sacred "monuments" in which their dead are solemnly interred. But it is a mere façade. The moral system which would give such a universe a credible substance manifests itself as an incoherent chaos. There is talk of "virtue" and "nobility," yet they appear to comprise nothing but a primitive valor in martial enterprise. "Piety" is named; but it gives nothing beyond a moment's historic authenticity to a Roman father's right to kill his son, and such historic authentication may even be an obstacle to dramatic plausibility: "the poet should prefer probable impossibilities to improbable possibilities."[3] In *Titus Andronicus* the standard of moral currency most in use is "honor." The word occurs a score of times in the scene in which Titus kills his son; it is made more prominent by another half-score instances of its opposite, "dishonor." But it is utterly impossible to define the content of the moral concept implied, and quite impossible therefore to assess its potency as a moral agent in motivating action. Titus is "dishonored" because his sons do not immediately obey his edict, and no less "dishonored" because Bassianus, with what appear to be highly honorable intentions, marries Titus' daughter. Saturninus is "dishonored" because someone has revealed the flagrant truth that he is a scoundrel, and even more "dishonored" because others have helped him to secure the throne in-

[3] *Ibid.*, XXIV, 10.

stead of recognizing his right to it without help. The audience, with more justice than Falstaff, may well inquire "what is this honor?" The play gives no answer, for nothing consistently recognizable as "honor" animates its action. Hence its incidents sink to melodrama. There are crucial examples in this first scene.

Take one which relies on an alleged ancient practice: the noblest prisoner taken must be sacrificed to appease "the groaning shadows of the slain." Tamora's son is the victim chosen by Titus' sons, and they will "hew his limbs and on a pile *Ad manes fratrum* sacrifice his flesh." Tamora appeals, with far less ancient terms and with more intelligible instinct, for the exercise of the "sweet mercy which is nobility's true badge." But Titus is placidly unmoved: for "their brethren slain" his sons "religiously ask a sacrifice"; they have marked her son for this, and "die he must." He is haled away by Titus' sons with fervent zeal, and in a twinkling they return to tell that his "limbs are lopped,"

> And entrails feed the sacrificing fire
> Whose smoke, like incense, doth perfume the sky.

As a mere record in human archaeology, such a scene can doubtless be freely paralleled; but its persons have not here inspired the psychological resuscitation which would give them dramatic personality. Their motives, therefore, implicit and explicit, are dramatically inert; the "must" of "die he must" is merely arbitrary and void of all power to excite in the audience a willing concurrence in its compulsiveness. Or take the incident in which Titus, exercising the Roman *jus patrium,* slays his son Mutius for a single act of sudden disobedience. Mutius' action is completely intelligible in common sense and in the simplest psychology; moreover, it commands enough moral sympathy to make it instantly credible to the audience. So, in despite of assurances from historical record, it is impossible for the audience to slip into a requisite and subconscious understanding of Titus. For them he is a lay figure, humanly, and therefore dramatically, unreal.

As in its first scene, so throughout the whole play. There is no inner world to it. Hence its plot is factitious; its people are mechanized puppets wearing masks of human faces, but seldom reacting even with a faint semblance of humanity except when their deeds are crimes which are prompted by a primitive human passion, crimes such as are still occasionally committed by the more bestial members of the human race. It is sheer melodrama and not tragedy; for, as *The New British Theatre* even as long ago as 1814 distinguished them, "in tragedy and comedy, the final event is the effect of the moral operations of the different characters, but in melodrama the catastrophe is the physical result of mechanical stratagem." And melodrama, lacking an inner world, can have none of the philosophic significance which is the peculiar function of tragedy; it can throw no light on the great mysteries of human fate.

RICHARD DAVID

Drams of Eale

Their virtues else—be they as pure as grace,
As infinite as man may undergo—
Shall in the general censure take corruption
From that particular fault: the dram of evil
Doth all the noble substance of a doubt
To his own scandal.

Hamlet's analysis applies to productions of Shakespeare as well as to men. The 1955–56 season promised marvels and in performance displayed an infinity of individual virtues. And yet the total impression was one of disappointment. There was always a dram of evil that finally undermined the most notable production.

Peter Brook's *Titus Andronicus* at Stratford (which came too late for inclusion in my last report) was certainly that. Brook had not only produced the play but had designed scenery, costumes, and musical accompaniment, and he achieved a quite extraordinary unity and concentration of effect. The staging was powerfully simple: three great squared pillars, set angle-on to the audience, fluted, and bronzy-gray in color. The two visible sides could be swung back, revealing inner recesses that might be used as entrances or, in the central pillar, as

From *Shakespeare Survey 10* (1957), edited by Allardyce Nicoll. Reprinted by permission of Cambridge University Press.

a two-storied inner stage. This was the tomb of the Andronici, somber and shadowy against the vivid green of the priests' robes and mushroom hats; festooned with lianes it became the murder pit and the forest floor above it; stained a yellowish natural-wood color, it provided a background of Roman frugality to the bereaved and brooding Titus at his family table; blood-red, it made a macabre eyrie of the upper chamber from which the Revenger peers out upon his victims, come in fantastic disguise to entrap him. In the court scenes the closed pillars, supported by heavy side gratings of the same color and hangings of purple and green, richly suggested the civilized barbarity of late imperial Rome.

Within this frame the whole phantasmagoria unrolled without hitch or hesitation—from the opening, when the citizens, in ruffed gowns of shot satin and dark fustian, broke off their rival acclamations to perform the obsequies for Titus' sons, marching and countermarching with obstinate purposefulness in a dirgelike quadrille; to the closing scene, when in the glare of the torches the victims topple forward in succession across the dinner table like a row of ninepins skittled from behind. It was as if the actors were engaged in a ritual at once fluent from habitual performance and yet still practiced with concentrated attention. There was something puppetlike about them; but puppets manipulated by a master whose genius for improvisation constantly enlivened his expert routine.

The compulsive and incantatory nature of the production (which sent some spectators off into faints before ever a throat was cut) was reinforced by the musical effects, all of a marvelous directness. The overture was a roll of drum and cymbal, the dirge for the slain Andronici, so strange and powerful, no more than the first two bars of *Three Blind Mice,* in the minor and endlessly repeated. A slow seesaw of two bass notes, a semitone apart, wrought the tension of the final scene to an unbearable pitch, and ceased abruptly, with breath-taking effect, as the first morsel of son-pie passed Tamora's lips. Even more harrowing were the hurrying carillon of electronic bells that led up to the abduction of Lavinia and the slow plucking of harp strings, like drops of blood falling into a pool, that accompanied her return to the stage.

In speaking of the actors as puppets of the producer's conception, I do not mean to imply that there were not performances of strong individuality but only that, like the dyer's hand, they were all loyally subdued to what they worked in. The freest, from the very nature of his part in the play, is Aaron the Moor, and to him Antony Quayle brought a rich gusto, as fetching in the creamy slyness that cheats Titus of his hand as in the bounce and glory of the defense of his black baby. But Aaron is a nice fat part for anyone; that Laurence Olivier should succeed in giving equal richness to the stock Revenger, Titus, was a more unexpected feat. At his first entry one might almost have accused him of mugging, so hard did he work with swallowing and pursing, wrinkling and charming to build up, on the bare bones of the part, a Great Man, cantankerous, choleric, and at the same time compelling. Yet by making Titus a "character," in every sense, he was able not only to gloss over some of the play's awkwardnesses but to rise (when, all too seldom, the chance was there) into a freer air than that of Grand Guignol. We could accept the conqueror's, and patriot's, blazing rage, that with "Barr'st me my way in Rome?" sweeps his youngest son out of existence. And the great central scene, where Titus stands

> as one upon a rock
> Environ'd with a wilderness of sea,
> Who marks the waxing tide grow wave by wave,

so grew and proliferated in the astonishing variety of his reactions to disaster (the enormous physical agony of the severed hand was almost unbearable) that with the crowning frenzy of "I am the sea" Olivier seemed to break through the illusion and become, not old Hieronimo run mad again, but madness itself.

As with individual performances, so with individual

scenes. Who could forget the return of the ravishers with Lavinia? They bring her through the leafy arch that was the central pillar and leave her standing there, right arm outstretched and head drooping away from it, left arm crooked with the wrist at her mouth. Her hair falls in disorder over face and shoulders, and from wrist and wrist-and-mouth trail scarlet streamers, symbols of her mutilation. The two assassins retreat from her, step by step, looking back at her, on either side of the stage. Their taunts fall softly, lingeringly, as if they themselves were in a daze at the horror of their deed; and the air tingles and reverberates with the slow plucking of harp strings. Another peak was the scene in which Titus makes his followers shoot arrows into the sky with messages for the gods. Here Brook cheated, bringing on the yokel, who seems to come in answer to the prayers, in a basket from the flies, and writing in a line about "fetching down his pigeons from the walls" to make this plausible. It was certainly in keeping, and added a crowning touch of fantasy to a most fantastical invention.

It was the whole, however, the one extended conjuring trick that held the spectator spellbound—spellbound and yet quite unmoved. What was it that in the last analysis made the evening so unrewarding, the effect so cold beside that of the perhaps more run-of-the-mill *Macbeth*? It was the conviction, unsought but growing irresistibly as the play proceeded, that this piece on which so much labor and ingenuity had been lavished, and to which we had been invited to attend for two and a half hours, was—twaddle. Perhaps this would have been less apparent if producer and company had not worked so hard to persuade us that it was otherwise. The Cambridge Marlowe Society's production in 1954, a shortened version played with frank gusto and dash, had prepared me to find in the play itself a straightforward blood-and-thunder entertainment. In striving to make it more than this Brook made it less than nothing. The blood was, we have seen, turned to favors and to prettiness. Severed heads were not allowed to appear unless decently swathed in black velvet and enclosed in ornate funerary caskets.

Titus' hand, so swaddled and coffered, was decorously cradled in Lavinia's arms, not carried off between her teeth as the text directs. The pig killing of Chiron and Demetrius occurred offstage and (perhaps to compensate the audience with one maiming in place of another) Titus' final cry of triumph,

> Why, there they are both, baked in that pie,

was lopped of its last four words. But no amount of sandpapering and gilding can turn this old shocker into high tragedy à la Racine. Has Shakespeare's *Titus* really any life left in it? The question is not yet answered. Certainly Brook's romantic play of the same name was stillborn.

Suggested References

The number of possible references is vast and grows alarmingly. (The *Shakespeare Quarterly* devotes a substantial part of one issue each year to a list of the previous year's work, and *Shakespeare Survey*—an annual publication—includes a substantial review of recent scholarship, as well as an occasional essay surveying a few decades of scholarship on a chosen topic.) Though no works are indispensable, those listed below have been found helpful.

1. Shakespeare's Times

Byrne, M. St. Clare. *Elizabethan Life in Town and Country*. Rev. ed. New York: Barnes & Noble, Inc., 1961. Chapters on manners, beliefs, education, etc., with illustrations.

Craig, Hardin. *The Enchanted Glass: the Elizabethan Mind in Literature*. New York and London: Oxford University Press, 1936. The Elizabethan intellectual climate.

Nicoll, Allardyce (ed.). *The Elizabethans*. London: Cambridge University Press, 1957. An anthology of Elizabethan writings, especially valuable for its illustrations from paintings, title pages, etc.

Shakespeare's England. 2 vols. Oxford: The Clarendon Press, 1916. A large collection of scholarly essays on a wide variety of topics (e.g., astrology, costume, gardening, horsemanship), with special attention to Shakespeare's references to these topics.

Tillyard, E. M. W. *The Elizabethan World Picture.* London: Chatto & Windus, 1943; New York: The Macmillan Company, 1944. A brief account of some Elizabethan ideas of the universe.

Wilson, John Dover (ed.). *Life in Shakespeare's England.* 2nd ed. New York: The Macmillan Company, 1913. An anthology of Elizabethan writings on the countryside, superstition, education, the court, etc.

2. Shakespeare

Bentley, Gerald E. *Shakespeare: A Biographical Handbook.* New Haven, Conn.: Yale University Press, 1961. The facts about Shakespeare, with virtually no conjecture intermingled.

Bradby, Anne (ed.). *Shakespeare Criticism, 1919–1935.* London: Oxford University Press, 1936. A small anthology of excellent essays on the plays.

Bush, Geoffrey Douglas. *Shakespeare and the Natural Condition.* Cambridge, Mass.: Harvard University Press; London: Oxford University Press, 1956. A short, sensitive account of Shakespeare's view of "Nature," touching most of the works.

Chambers, E. K. *William Shakespeare: A Study of Facts and Problems.* 2 vols. London: Oxford University Press, 1930. An invaluable, detailed reference work; not for the casual reader.

Chute, Marchette. *Shakespeare of London.* New York: E. P. Dutton & Co., Inc., 1949. A readable biography fused with portraits of Stratford and London life.

Clemen, Wolfgang H. *The Development of Shakespeare's Imagery.* Cambridge, Mass.: Harvard University Press,

1951. (Originally published in German, 1936.) A temperate account of a subject often abused.

Craig, Hardin. *An Interpretation of Shakespeare.* New York: Citadel Press, 1948. A scholar's book designed for the layman. Comments on all the works.

Dean, Leonard F. (ed.). *Shakespeare: Modern Essays in Criticism.* New York: Oxford University Press, 1957. Mostly mid-twentieth-century critical studies, covering Shakespeare's artistry.

Granville-Barker, Harley. *Prefaces to Shakespeare.* 2 vols. Princeton, N.J.: Princeton University Press, 1946–47. Essays on ten plays by a scholarly man of the theater.

Harbage, Alfred. *As They Liked It.* New York: The Macmillan Company, 1947. A sensitive, long essay on Shakespeare, morality, and the audience's expectations.

Ridler, Anne Bradby (ed.). *Shakespeare Criticism, 1935–1960.* New York and London: Oxford University Press, 1963. An excellent continuation of the anthology edited earlier by Miss Bradby (see above).

Smith, D. Nichol (ed.). *Shakespeare Criticism.* New York: Oxford University Press, 1916. A selection of criticism from 1623 to 1840, ranging from Ben Jonson to Thomas Carlyle.

Spencer, Theodore, *Shakespeare and the Nature of Man.* New York: The Macmillan Company, 1942. Shakespeare's plays in relation to Elizabethan thought.

Stoll, Elmer Edgar. *Shakespeare and Other Masters.* Cambridge, Mass.: Harvard University Press; London: Oxford University Press, 1940. Essays on tragedy, comedy, and aspects of dramaturgy, with special reference to some of Shakespeare's plays.

Traversi, D. A. *An Approach to Shakespeare.* Rev. ed. New York: Doubleday & Co., Inc., 1956. An analysis of the plays, beginning with words, images, and themes, rather than with characters.

Van Doren, Mark. *Shakespeare*. New York: Henry Holt & Company, Inc., 1939. Brief, perceptive readings of al of the plays.

Whitaker, Virgil K. *Shakespeare's Use of Learning*. San Marino, Calif.: Huntington Library, 1953. A study of the relation of Shakespeare's reading to his development as a dramatist.

3. Shakespeare's Theater

Adams, John Cranford. *The Globe Playhouse*. Rev. ed. New York: Barnes & Noble, Inc., 1961. A detailed conjecture about the physical characteristics of the theater Shakespeare often wrote for.

Beckerman, Bernard. *Shakespeare at the Globe, 1599–1609*. New York: The Macmillan Company, 1962. On the playhouse and on Elizabethan dramaturgy, acting, and staging.

Chambers, E. K. *The Elizabethan Stage*. 4 vols. New York: Oxford University Press, 1923. Reprinted with corrections, 1945. An indispensable reference work on theaters, theatrical companies, and staging at court.

Harbage, Alfred. *Shakespeare's Audience*. New York: Columbia University Press; London: Oxford University Press, 1941. A study of the size and nature of the theatrical public.

Hodges, C. Walter. *The Globe Restored*. London: Ernest Benn, Ltd., 1953; New York: Coward-McCann, Inc., 1954. A well-illustrated and readable attempt to reconstruct the Globe Theatre.

Nagler, A. M. *Shakespeare's Stage*. Tr. by Ralph Manheim. New Haven, Conn.: Yale University Press, 1958. An excellent brief introduction to the physical aspect of the playhouse.

Smith, Irwin. *Shakespeare's Globe Playhouse*. New York: Charles Scribner's Sons, 1957. Chiefly indebted to J. C. Adams' controversial book, with additional material and scale drawings for model-builders.

Venezky, Alice S. *Pageantry on the Shakespearean Stage*. New York: Twayne Publishers, Inc., 1951. An examination of spectacle in Elizabethan drama.

4. Miscellaneous Reference Works

Abbott, E. A. *A Shakespearean Grammar*. New edition. New York: The Macmillan Company, 1877. An examination of differences between Elizabethan and modern grammar.

Bartlett, John. *A New and Complete Concordance . . . to . . . Shakespeare*. New York: The Macmillan Company, 1894. An index to most of Shakespeare's words.

Bullough, Geoffrey. *Narrative and Dramatic Sources of Shakespeare*. 4 vols. Vols. 5 and 6 in preparation. New York: Columbia University Press; London: Routledge & Kegan Paul, Ltd., 1957–. A collection of many of the books Shakespeare drew upon.

Greg, W. W. *The Shakespeare First Folio*. New York and London: Oxford University Press, 1955. A detailed yet readable history of the first collection (1623) of Shakespeare's plays.

Kökeritz, Helge. *Shakespeare's Names*. New Haven, Conn.: Yale University Press, 1959; London: Oxford University Press, 1960. A guide to the pronunciation of some 1,800 names appearing in Shakespeare.

———. *Shakespeare's Pronunciation*. New Haven, Conn.: Yale University Press; London: Oxford University Press, 1953. Contains much information about puns and rhymes.

Linthicum, Marie C. *Costume in the Drama of Shakespeare and His Contemporaries*. New York and London: Oxford University Press, 1936. On the fabrics and dress of the age, and references to them in the plays.

Muir, Kenneth. *Shakespeare's Sources*. London: Methuen & Co., Ltd., 1957. Vol. 2 in preparation. The first volume, on the comedies and tragedies, attempts to ascertain what books were Shakespeare's sources, and what use he made of them.

Onions, C. T. *A Shakespeare Glossary*. London: Oxford University Press, 1911; 2nd ed., rev., with enlarged addenda, 1953. Definitions of words (or senses of words) now obsolete.

Partridge, Eric. *Shakespeare's Bawdy*. Rev. ed. New York: E. P. Dutton & Co., Inc.; London: Routledge & Kegan Paul, Ltd., 1955. A glossary of bawdy words and phrases.

Shakespeare Quarterly. See headnote to Suggested References.

Shakespeare Survey. See headnote to Suggested References.

Smith, Gordon Ross. *A Classified Shakespeare Bibliography, 1936–1958*. University Park, Pa.: Pennsylvania State University Press, 1963. A list of some 20,000 items on Shakespeare.

5. *Titus Andronicus*

Baker, Howard. *Induction to Tragedy*. Baton Rouge: Louisiana State University Press, 1939.

Findlater, Richard. "Shakespearean Atrocities," *Twentieth Century*, CLVIII (1955), 364–72.

Hamilton, A. C. *"Titus Andronicus;* The Form of Shakespearian Tragedy," *Shakespeare Quarterly,* XIV (1963), 201–13.

Hill, R. F. "The Composition of *Titus Andronicus,"* *Shakespeare Survey 10,* ed. Allardyce Nicoll. New York and London: Cambridge University Press, 1957, pp. 60–70.

Ribner, Irving. *Patterns in Shakespearean Tragedy*. New York: Barnes & Noble, Inc.; London: Methuen & Co., Ltd., 1960.

Sargent, Ralph M. "The Source of *Titus Andronicus*," *Studies in Philology*, XLVI (1949), 167–83.

Sommers, Alan. " 'Wilderness of Tigers': Structure and Symbolism in *Titus Andronicus*," *Essays in Criticism*, X (1960), 275–89.

Spencer, T. J. B. *Shakespeare: The Roman Plays*. New York: British Book Centre, Inc.; London: Longmans, Green & Co., Ltd., 1963.

Spivack, Bernard. *Shakespeare and the Allegory of Evil*. New York: Columbia University Press; London: Oxford University Press, 1958.

Tynan, Kenneth. *Curtains*. New York: Atheneum Publishers, 1961.

Waith, Eugene M. "The Metamorphosis of Violence in *Titus Andronicus*," *Shakespeare Survey 10,* ed. Allardyce Nicoll. New York and London: Cambridge University Press, 1957, pp. 39–49.

THE COMPLETE PLAYS OF
SHAKESPEARE

Superlatively edited paperbound volumes of Shakespeare's complete plays are now being added to the Signet Classic list. Under the general editorship of Sylvan Barnet, Chairman of the English Department of Tufts University, each volume will feature a general Introduction by Dr. Barnet; special Introduction and Notes by an eminent Shakespearean scholar; critical commentary from past and contemporary authorities, and when possible, the actual source, in its entirety or in excerpt, from which Shakespeare derived his play. The first volumes, priced at only 50 cents each, include:

KING LEAR. EDITED WITH INTRODUCTION AND NOTES BY RUSSELL FRASER, PRINCETON UNIVERSITY. CD160

MACBETH. EDITED WITH INTRODUCTION AND NOTES BY SYLVAN BARNET, TUFTS UNIVERSITY. CD161

OTHELLO. EDITED WITH INTRODUCTION AND NOTES BY ALVIN KERNAN, YALE UNIVERSITY. CD162

RICHARD II. EDITED WITH INTRODUCTION AND NOTES BY KENNETH MUIR, UNIVERSITY OF LIVERPOOL. CD163

THE WINTER'S TALE. EDITED WITH INTRODUCTION AND NOTES BY FRANK KERMODE, UNIVERSITY OF MANCHESTER. CD164

AS YOU LIKE IT. EDITED WITH INTRODUCTION AND NOTES BY ALBERT GILMAN, BOSTON UNIVERSITY. CD168

HAMLET. EDITED WITH INTRODUCTION AND NOTES BY EDWARD HUBLER, PRINCETON UNIVERSITY. CD169

JULIUS CAESAR. EDITED WITH INTRODUCTION AND NOTES BY WILLIAM AND BARBARA ROSEN, UNIVERSITY OF CONNECTICUT. CD170

A MIDSUMMER NIGHT'S DREAM. EDITED WITH INTRODUCTION AND NOTES BY WOLFGANG CLEMEN, UNIVERSITY OF MUNICH. CD171

TROILUS AND CRESSIDA. EDITED WITH INTRODUCTION AND NOTES BY DANIEL SELTZER, HARVARD UNIVERSITY. CD172

OTHER SIGNET CLASSICS

JANE EYRE *by Charlotte Bronte*
The famous romantic novel of the love of the plain but courageous governess and the brooding, melancholy Rochester. Afterword by Arthur Zeiger.
(#CD11—50¢)

GULLIVER'S TRAVELS *by Jonathan Swift*
The four classic voyages of Gulliver, which make both a fascinating fairy tale and a bitter satire. With 30 illustrations by Charles Brock and 5 maps. Foreword by Marcus Cunliffe.
(#CD14—50¢)

FABLES AND FAIRY TALES *by Leo Tolstoy*
26 folk tales by the great Russian novelist, illustrated by Sheila Greenwald. Newly translated by Ann Dunnigan with a Foreword by Raymond Rosenthal.
(#CP132—60¢)

LEAVES OF GRASS *by Walt Whitman*
Whitman's enduring testament to a land whose vitality was the touchstone of his genius. A complete edition with an Introduction by Gay Wilson Allen, the Whitman authority.
(#CT23—75¢)

THE CELTIC TWILIGHT AND A SELECTION OF EARLY POEMS *by William Butler Yeats*
Mystic tales and poems based on the legends of his native land, by the great Irish poet. Foreword by Walter Starkie.
(#CP120—60¢)

ANNA KARENINA *by Leo Tolstoy*
This classic love story also contains the nucleus of Tolstoy's philosophy. Newly translated and with an Intruction by David Magarshack.
(#CQ34—95¢)

THE COSSACKS AND THE RAID *by Leo Tolstoy*
Two powerful stories by the Russian master, newly translated by Andrew R. MacAndrew. Afterword by F. D. Reeve.
(#CD56—50¢)

DEIRDRE *by James Stephens*
A haunting allegorical novel based on a violent, primordial Gaelic legend. Afterword by Walter Starkie.
(#CP116—60¢)

THE TRAVELS OF MARCO POLO

The enduring record of Marco Polo's thirty-five years of fabulous Eastern travel. Edited with an Introduction by Milton Rugoff. (#CD97—50¢)

THE INFORMER by Liam O'Flaherty

This story of a hunted man who has betrayed his friend to the enemy presents a harshly realistic picture of Ireland divided by the Civil War in the 1920's. Afterword by Donagh McDonagh. (#CP80—60¢)

CANDIDE, ZADIG and Selected Stories by Voltaire

Voltaire satirizes with ruthless wit the social, religious, and human vanities of his day in sixteen biting stories. A new translation with an Introduction by Donald Frame. (#CD35—50¢)

RESURRECTION by Leo Tolstoy

The Russian master's final work tells the story of a young man who seeks salvation by following into exile the girl for whose career in crime he was responsible. Translated by Vera Traill with a Foreword by Alan Hodge. (#CT63—75¢)

OLIVER TWIST by Charles Dickens

Dickins' classic indictment of the orphanages and crime-ridden slums of 19th Century London. Afterword by Edward Le Comte. (#CP102—60¢)

PLATERO AND I by Juan Ramon Jiménez

The delightful tale of a poet and his playful donkey by one of Spain's great Nobel Prize winning authors. Translated by William and Mary Roberts, with an Introduction by William Roberts. (#CD17—50¢)

THE SCARLET LETTER by Nathaniel Hawthorne

A masterpiece by one of America's fine 19th Century writers, this is the story of a proud and sinful woman in Puritan New England. Foreword by Leo Marx.

(#CD8—50¢)